WE SAVED YOU A SEAT

Finding and Keeping Lasting Friendships

(in)courage community manager

LISA-JO BAKER

LifeWay Press®
Nashville, Tennessee

Published by LifeWay Press® • ©2017 DaySpring Cards, Inc.

Reprinted April 2020

ISBN 978-1-4300-5496-2
Item 006103971
Dewey decimal classification: 231.7
Subject heading: FRIENDSHIP \ SPIRITUAL LIFE \ JESUS CHRIST

To order additional copies of this resource, write LifeWay Church Resources Customer Service; One LifeWay Plaza; Nashville, TN 37234-0113; FAX order to 615.251.5933; call toll-free 800.458.2772; email *orderentry@lifeway.com;* or order online at *www.lifeway.com.*

Printed in the United States of America

Adult Ministry Publishing, LifeWay Church Resources, One LifeWay Plaza, Nashville, TN 37234-0152

Author is represented by Alive Literary Agency, 7680 Goddard Street, Suite 200, Colorado Springs, CO 80920, *www.aliveliterary.com.*

TABLE OF CONTENTS

ABOUT THE AUTHOR

LISA-JO BAKER

Lisa-Jo Baker has been the community manager for *www.incourage.me*, an online home for women all over the world, for nearly a decade. She is the author of *Never Unfriended* and *Surprised by Motherhood*, as well as the creator of *The Temper Toolkit*, and her writings have been syndicated from New Zealand to New York. She lives just outside Washington, DC, with her husband and their three very loud kids, where she connects, encourages, and champions women in person and through her blog, *lisajobaker.com*. She is convinced that the shortest distance between strangers is a shared awkward story, and she'd love to connect with you on Twitter®, Facebook®, or Instagram® @lisajobaker.

At (in)courage you are welcome to a place of faith, connection, and friendship, where you will always find yourself among friends. Founded in 2009 by DaySpring, the Christian products subsidiary of Hallmark Cards, Inc., the vision for (in)courage was to create a new home for the hearts of women, where women take turns pulling up a chair to share their stories of what Jesus looks like in their everyday, gloriously ordinary, and often messy lives. Since then, (in)courage has grown into a vibrant community that reaches thousands of women every day, welcoming them just the way they are, offering a space to breathe, loving support, and resources for meaningful connection.

ABOUT THE VIDEO PARTICIPANTS

ALIA JOY

Alia Joy is a writer, speaker, and home-schooling mother of three making her home in Central Oregon with her husband, Josh, her tiny Asian mother, a dog, a bunny, and a bunch of chickens. She shares her life with readers of her blog, *aliajoy.com,* where she believes some of the most powerful words are "me too." She writes so people will know they're not alone and that God is good even when life gets messy. She is also a regular monthly contributor at (in)courage, SheLoves Magazine, GraceTable, The Mudroom, and Deeper Waters. Find her on Instagram @AliaJoy.

ALIZA LATTA

Aliza Latta is a Canadian writer, journalist, and artist, who is a huge fan of telling stories—whether through speech, written prose, or art. She writes about faith and young adulthood on her blog, *alizanaomi.com,* and creates hand-lettered prints for her online shop, *etsy.com/shop/choosebrave.* Find her on Twitter or Instagram as @alizalatta.

DEIDRA RIGGS

Deidra Riggs is the visionary behind life-changing events for writers, artists, entrepreneurs, and other fabulous people who have an amazing dream. She is the author of *Every Little Thing: Making a World of Difference Right Where You Are* and *ONE: Unity in a Divided World.* Through her engaging and relatable talks, practical and inspiring books, and first-class events, she works to cross cultural boundaries, build bridges with those who are different, and create more peace in the world while making it all feel like a fabulous celebration of life. When she's not inspiring people to live life to the fullest and push past invisible boundaries, you can find her frolicking in the ocean, dancing to loud disco tunes, or hosting a group of her closest friends around the dinner table.

KRISTEN STRONG

Kristen Strong is wife to her retired Air Force veteran, mama to three priority blessings, and fresh-air giver to you. She is the author of *Girl Meets Change,* a book that helps women see their difficult life change in a more hopeful light. Kristen writes regularly at *chasingblueskies.net* and once a month at DaySpring's *incourage.me* to encourage women to see themselves as Jesus does. She and her family zigzagged across the country (and one ocean!) several times before settling in Colorado Springs. Kristen would love to connect with you on her favorite social media site Instagram as @kristenstrong.

WHY SHOULD YOU DO A BIBLE STUDY ABOUT FRIENDSHIP?

Because I don't know anyone who doesn't want friends. But I know lots of women who worry about being unfriended. Or misunderstood. Or hurt or judged or left out or taken for granted by their friends. I'm one of them.

So they stop trying. They stop risking. They stop starting over. Because they've stopped believing there'll be a seat saved for them at the table—at the book club, the PTA meeting, the Bible study, the office break room, the retreat, the lunch date, the church pew, or the living room sofa of the women who used to be their best friends.

That's what this study is about. It's about not giving up on friendship. Even when we're frustrated by it. Even when we're tired of it, confused by it, or disappointed in it. This is a chance to change that.

This is a practical guide to finding and keeping lasting friendships.

This is believing that there really is a seat saved for you at the table. And it's also about becoming the kind of women who will always save a seat for the women around them.

Because, the ultimate friend, Jesus—the one who moved into the neighborhood and pulled up a chair to get to know us, the friend of the popular and unpopular, of priests and pastors, of the educated and the uneducated, of elementary school girls and their minivan driving moms—put it pretty plain and simple. When asked what the greatest commandment was, He said,

> Love the Lord your God with all your heart, with all your soul, and with all your mind. This is the greatest and most important command. The second is like it: **Love your neighbor as yourself. All the Law and the Prophets depend on these two commands.**
> MATTHEW 22:36-40 (EMPHASIS MINE)

And when pressed to define who exactly this neighbor is that we're commanded to love, He didn't give an inch. He gave a story. And it defines neighbor not as a particular "who," but instead as a "what": as in *what* you should *do*. The parable of the good Samaritan isn't about identifying your neighbor; it's about *being* a neighbor. In essence, it's about being the kind of friend you wish you had.

While we might have defined friendship our whole lives by what others do to us, in the end it's what we do for others that will define us as friends or not. That's how we get friendship to stick. And that's what this study is about.

Together we will unpack what that kind of friendship takes—seven practical ways to take Jesus up on His invitation to love other people. To be friends who go first, who make the first move—and sometimes the hundredth move—of starting over. This is the meat and potatoes of life—figuring out how to get along with the people we love as well as the ones who rub us the wrong way. This is the whole shebang explored in seven simple steps.

Here's how it's going to work:

- Gather some friends to watch each video session or enjoy tuning in from the comfort of your own home.

- Use the Viewer Guide to process the video discussion.

- Spend the next week working through three days of Bible study to dig deeper into what it takes to find and keep lasting friendships.

- Circle back together again to discuss what you learned the past week, watch the next video, and dig deeper into the content throughout the week. Repeat.

Let's do this together.

Lisa-Jo

THE
cardinal
rule of
FRIENDSHIP
is you have to
BE WILLING
to go FIRST.

FRIENDSHIP TAKES SHOWING UP

For God loved the world in this way: He gave his one and only Son, so that everyone who believes in him will not perish but have eternal life.

JOHN 3:16

Friendship TAKES Showing up

VIEWER GUIDE: SESSION 1

Watch the Session 1 video and discuss with your group the following questions:

1. Why do you think it's so difficult to make lasting friendships as women?

2. Read James 3:18 in The Message paraphrase. (Read multiple translations if you can.) What does James say about our personal responsibility in friendship?

3. Lisa-Jo explained in the video, "God breathed into our DNA the need for community." How have you seen this truth in your own life? How do you think we've been hardwired for authentic friendships?

4. Alia noted how easy it is to be lonely, even within a church group. How have you experienced loneliness even in the midst of the group?

5. Why is authentic conversation (beyond "I'm fine") difficult at times for you or others?

6. Discuss how we can enter into more authentic and personal conversations instead of settling for superficial answers such as "I'm fine."

7. What are some excuses we use not to show up (i.e., "I'm too busy.")?

8. Aliza described loving friends in *their* best way. Describe a time when you have failed or succeeded in loving someone in *her* best way. Why is this important?

9. Describe examples of how Jesus loved people in *their* best way.

10. With your group, highlight any meaningful truths you took away from today's conversation at the table.

Video sessions available for purchase
at *LifeWay.com/WeSavedYouASeat*

BELIEVE WHAT GOD SAYS ABOUT FRIENDSHIP

Can you be convinced that nothing could make the God who gave up His title, His throne, His realm, and His only Son for you ever consider unfriending you? No matter how crabby you are, how tired, frustrated, or unloving?

Because that's where we need to start, at the beginning of the first friendship: God's friendship with the human beings He created. This is the road map for all future friendships.

What if I told you that neither Facebook nor church cliques, friendship breakups nor family disapproval, bad moods nor all your undone to-dos will ever be able to separate us from the radical, never-giving-up, never-looking-back love of God? God's love proved itself when it took deep breaths in the flesh and blood of Jesus Christ, who literally moved into the neighborhood so that He could be up close and personal friends with *you* and who has promised that He will never leave you nor forsake you.

Would you believe me?

What is going through your head right now? Because I know that talking about friendship can stir up a lot of feelings and a lot of memories—both good and bad. So, let's unpack some of those. What's the first thing that comes to mind when you think about friendship? Just write it down here without editing yourself. It's OK to be brutally honest.

When I think about friendship, I feel:

When I think about friendship, I remember:

I don't know about you, but when I think about friendship my stomach can knot up. Sure, I feel warm and fuzzy about it on some days. I have close friends who wrap me in safety and loving acceptance. But when I really think about it, the idea of friendship can spark hundreds of hard memories. Evenings spent awkwardly trying not to cry in hotel lobbies or panic checking my phone in the middle of the night or trying to act like it's no big deal when I'm not invited to the same event I wasn't invited to last year.

Friendship is not easy. It's not always fun. It's rarely like the commercials or "squad goals" photos the ad world or online world would like us to believe. Because nothing hurts quite like the unkind words of a friend, even the careless words that weren't intended to cut can leave scars. And I know I'm not the only one who feels this way.

I've heard too many stories, cried with too many women, and apologized too many times to think I'm the only one with these bruises on my heart and holes in my story where friends fell through.

I'm guessing you can relate.

I'm guessing there are days you just want to be done with it all. It feels like too much extra work when your plate is already full and you're already juggling a circus of commitments. You don't need one more to-do, especially from a person who wants nothing to do with you. It's so much easier to just chuck it and be done with it all.

But here's the thing—I believe that it is both physically and spiritually impossible to simply wash our hands of other people.

As much as you might try to quit it, friendship is literally woven into your bones. With every breath you take, about 20 breaths per minute, you are entirely dependent on the life breathed into you by a God whose entire existence is a living, breathing friendship of three. He has designed friendship into your DNA, so trying to cut friendship out of your life is like trying to cut a piece of yourself out of yourself. It will hurt. It will leave open wounds. I hope I can convince you that it's not worth it—and that it's not healthy for your soul.

Who is the very first character we meet in the Bible?

Many scholars believe that the Hebrew word used to name this character in the first verse is *Elohim*. This is significant because *Elohim* is the *plural* form of that Hebrew word.

In the next few chapters of Genesis, God refers to Himself in the plural form twice more.

READ GENESIS 1:26a AND GENESIS 3:22a.

What are the two pronouns God uses to refer to Himself in these verses?

From the very first sentences of the story of God and the people He created we are introduced to Him as a holy friendship that we call the Trinity—one God, in three different Persons. Those three parts of God might be as familiar to you as your own name or they might be a brand new idea. Either way, let's read 2 Corinthians 13:13 (depending on your Bible translation, you may need to also consult verse 14) and write down each of the three Persons who make up our one God as well as the character trait Paul associates with each of them:

1. The _____ of _____

2. The _____ of _____

3. The _____ of the _____

Genesis is the first place we get to overhear God having a conversation with Himself. And this won't be the last time. Throughout Jesus' life we will get to overhear God the Son having conversations with God the Father, and we will hear God the Son talking about God the Holy Spirit.

One of the most poignant times we get to listen in on the friendship between our three-in-one God is the tender moment of Jesus' baptism—where all three Persons of the Trinity are specifically mentioned.

LET'S READ MATTHEW 3:13-17 AND IDENTIFY EACH PART OF THE TRINITY AND WHAT THEY EACH SAID/DID:

"When _____ was baptized, he went up immediately from the water. The heavens suddenly opened for him, and he saw the _____ descending like a _____ and coming down on him. And a voice from heaven said:

'This is my _____ _____, with whom I am well-pleased'" (vv. 16-17).

The profound tenderness and holy joy that ripples through that moment can give you goosebumps. Here is blessing and friendship and benediction and delight all wrapped up into a single recorded moment in history. This is God publicly celebrating and delighting in the most sacred of relationships—His own.

We have been modeled on and built out of that DNA, made in an image that bears the permanent mark of friendship. We are intended for friendship with God and friendship with each other. But from the very beginning, Satan has tried to burn that image out of us.

Once Satan spewed his first temptation and Adam and Eve doubted God and then disobeyed Him, we see the backlash of our broken relationship with God ripping through history. From Adam and Eve, to Cain and Abel, to Noah and his community, to Abraham and Lot, to Saul and David, to Mary and Martha, to the squabbling disciples and down through our biblical family tree to you and me, Satan is on a campaign to convince us to doubt God and distrust each other.

But our faithful God has been just as determined to keep putting back together the original friendship that got broken. The entire story of Scripture hinges on how Jesus has come to restore our relationships, first with God and second with each other. In the verse that is the heartbeat of God's friendship with us we read:

> For God loved the world in this way: He gave his one and only Son, so that everyone who believes in him will not perish but have eternal life.
> JOHN 3:16

It's the entire reason why Jesus was on earth and available to be baptized. He came to make things right so that we could live at peace with God as well as with the other human beings God created and placed in our lives.

LET'S READ FROM COLOSSIANS TOGETHER:

He [Jesus] is the beginning,
the firstborn from the dead,
so that he might come to have
first place in everything.
For God was pleased to have
all his fullness dwell in him,
and through him to reconcile
everything to himself
whether things on earth or things in heaven,
by making peace
through his blood, shed on the cross.
COLOSSIANS 1:18b-20 (EMPHASIS MINE)

Everything. Every single broken heart, every twisted family tie, every crushed spirit and wounded relationship, every single thing that has breath to breathe and tears to cry—*everything* is able and intended to be reconciled to God through His Son, Jesus Christ. Such is His wild and wonderful love for us, the creatures created in His image.

And in the final conversation Jesus the Son had with God the Father before He was betrayed and crucified we get to hear firsthand how passionately Jesus feels about that assignment.

In one of His final prayers before He was crucified, some of Jesus' very last words to His Father were about His friends—the people entrusted to Him. What did He say about them?

GO AND READ JOHN 17:6-19.

Jesus could tell His Father, in no uncertain terms, that as far as it was possible for Him, He had kept the faith and the friendship of every one of the friends entrusted to Him. Even Judas had been included right up until the moment He chose to quit Jesus, not the other way around.

If you have a highlighter, please highlight or underline verse 12 in your Bible.

Now put your own name into the verse:

"While I was with _____, I was protecting [her] by your name that you have given me. I guarded _____ ..." (John 17:12).

When you hear the word *protected* what does it bring to mind? Write down a few words you associate with the idea of being "protected."

When you hear the word *guarded* what does it bring to mind? Write down a few words you associate with the idea of being "guarded."

Both words are significant cornerstones of what it means to be God's friend. The commentaries spend a lot of time unpacking the power of these words. *Protection* gives us the image of a shepherd tenderly caring for and feeding his flock, while *guarding* implies the kind of actions that would bravely protect you from all kinds of wild beasts determined to rip your life to shreds.[1]

Taking the image even further, the Greek word Jesus used when he talked about guarding His disciples meant the kind of protection you'd get "behind the walls of a fortress."[2] Those are the very walls Jesus wraps around you—to guard and protect you by His Holy Spirit. You are so dear to Him. He is the friend who gave up His very life to protect you. He is the friend who lived up to His own definition of love and friendship.

Write it down here from John 15:13:

"No one has greater love than this: _____
_____."

He is the friend who is with you, protecting you, and guarding you, even with His very own life.

Now think of the people in your life. Picture the faces of your friends—even the ones who have frustrated, irritated, or hurt you. Can you put them into this sentence?

"While I was with _____, I was protecting [her] by your name that you have given me. I guarded _____ ..." (John 17:12).

Can you do that? Are you willing to be a safe place for them—a friend who will offer the walls of protection and compassion like a fortress around them?

That's what this study is about—believing that we are safely guarded by Jesus' friendship and, secondly, being willing to put our friends—the people trusted to us—into John 17:12. We can't guard and protect our friends in the way that Jesus guards and protects His followers, but we're called to become a guard around their lives with real friendship. A friendship that doesn't hold back and prays for them. A friendship that always believes the best about them and wants the best for them because we're convinced that is how serious God is about His friendship with us. Ultimately, we want to be like Jesus. We want to be willing to lay down our lives for our friends (John 15:13).

But until we have that truth cemented into the foundation of our identity, we will not be able to give that kind of friendship to other people.

For that kind of friendship to be possible you need to believe it first for yourself. So as we get started on this journey together, please take this truth and deposit it—use superglue if necessary—into the very core of who you are: **Jesus guarded His friends—that includes you and me—with His very life.**

FRIENDSHIP CHALLENGE

At the end of every day, we will take a Friendship Challenge. This will help you apply what we've learned to your own life and relationships. Today, write out this verse and stick it above your mirror, on your car's dashboard, in your closet, or as the screen saver on your phone so that you can begin to superglue its truth to your soul. Be sure to put your own name, as well as the name of at least one friend, in the blanks:

> "While I was with _____, I was protecting [her] by your name that you have given me. I guarded _____ ..." (John 17:12).

Use the additional space on this page and other Friendship Challenge pages to jot down things that you've learned.

BE WILLING TO BE INTERRUPTED

If you ask people how they're doing these days you'll likely hear one of two responses: "I'm fine" or "I'm so busy." We live in a world where politeness trumps honesty and productivity trumps rest. So the last thing anyone expects to hear in response to the question, "How are you?" is the truth. Because some days that might sound like, "I'm crazy excited about my new promotion," "I'm so smitten with my new baby," or "I'm enjoying a quiet afternoon off."

But, there are other answers that are harder to share, so we tend to shove them deep down inside of us where they can't slip out and shock anyone: *I'm exhausted. I'm depressed. I don't think I can stand being a mom for another minute. I'm overwhelmed. I'm lonely. I'm still grieving. I'm maxed out,* or *I'm about to lose my mind.* It feels awkward to interrupt someone else's day by shoving onto them the unexpected baggage of how we're *actually* doing. It feels like an inconvenience. An interruption. An imposition on their time.

So we get really good about faking fine and keeping our baggage tucked neatly away so that it doesn't spill over into the lives and afternoons of the people around us. That would be embarrassing and awkward because what happens when you tell someone how you're really doing and they don't have time for it?

If there's one thing that defined Jesus' time on earth it was His willingness to be interrupted. And not just that there were constant interruptions (and good grief there were a ridiculous amount of those!), what's so striking is how instead of being annoyed by them, He *welcomed* them.

Let's compare how we feel/act about interruptions to how Jesus responded to being interrupted.

First, make a list of how *you* think *other people* will react if you interrupt their day to tell them how you're *really* doing and ask for help instead of just giving the default answer of, "I'm fine." (I've filled in the first two to get you started.)

I'm worried that if I tell people how I'm really doing they will feel:
Inconvenienced
Embarrassed

Now make a list of how you might react if someone interrupted *your* day to tell you how they're really doing and to ask for help.

If someone else shared how she was really doing, instead of just saying she was "fine," I'd feel:
Surprised
Nervous

Now let's spend some time with Jesus to see how His days and His interruptions looked. Read the verses and answer the questions at the top of the following chart. If we trace several days in Jesus' life as chronicled by His disciples, Matthew and Mark, this is what we find:

Verses	Where was Jesus going?	Who interrupted Him?	What did they want?	What did Jesus do?
Matthew 8:5-13	To the city of Capernaum			
Matthew 8:14-15	To Peter's house			
Matthew 8:18, 23-27	To the other side of the Sea of Galilee			
Matthew 8:28-34	To the region of the Gadarenes			
Matthew 9:1-8	Back across the sea to His own town (Capernaum)			
Matthew 9:18-19,23-26	To teach His disciples			
Matthew 9:20-22	To Jairus' house			
Matthew 9:27-30	He "went on from there" (from Jairus' house) to another house			
Mark 10:46-52	Leaving Jericho			
Matthew 19:13-15	To teach His disciples			

Jesus stopped *every single time*. He allowed Himself to be interrupted, detoured, and inconvenienced. It's never the perfect time and never in a perfect setting. This is eye-opening for me—the woman intimidated by Pinterest® who has been known to shove dirty dishes into the microwave and/or hide in the bedroom when unexpected visitors stop by—because by Sunday afternoons our house often looks like a circus passed through with every surface covered in teetering stacks of dishes or piles of laundry, and shoes, swimsuits, socks, pens, and pencils flung every which way around the front door and in a chaotic trail down the hall.

If I'm being super forthcoming, I've even sweated the planned visits. I admit I like the perfectly-planned setting, food, kid behavior, and a visit that has a set start and end time. For years I would have described myself as a "reluctant renter." We were married 17 years before we bought our first house. And one of our longest rentals was small, grubby, and had faux bricks that constantly fell off the kitchen walls and carpets that, well, let's just say back then we had three kids under the age of five and leave the rest up to your imagination.

For years my small, terribly imperfect house stunted my hospitality.

But the thing is, being willing to be interrupted isn't about the state of our houses. It's about the state of our hearts. Women aren't hungry for perfection; they're hungry for connection. One of the ways our world of the fast and furious Internet hurts us is that so often our schedules and attention spans don't have enough time to give each other uninterrupted hours of conversation. But we will starve on a diet of conversations limited to 140 character tweets, text messages, or Facebook quips. We need soul food conversations. The kind that don't cut you off because they have another appointment to run to. The kind that lingers.

I learned this the hard way through a selfish, split-second moment when I wasn't willing to make time for a friend—when I wasn't willing to be interrupted, when I wasn't willing to linger. And I would take it back if I could. But I can't because my dear friend passed away a couple weeks after the night I avoided her.

I remember it with a knot in my stomach. It was a night when I was tired and our kids were being wild and unruly after a late night church event. All I wanted was to wrangle everyone back into the minivan, to home, and to bed. I wanted my shoes off, my hair down, and my comfy pants on. And as I was crossing through the church hall, I kept my eyes down so that I wouldn't have to stumble into conversation with anyone.

I wove my way through the chairs trying to get to my kids and spotted one of my Tuesday night Bible study girls with her back to me and her hand on her cane. Without even giving it a second thought I backtracked around her so that I wouldn't have to pause to talk. So that I wouldn't have to give up a second of my time to a friend who lived by herself in a small room with her cats and her passion for beautiful, colorful necklaces and who came out every Tuesday night because she was so hungry for company.

Just a few weeks later she had a stroke that she never recovered from. She died before there was a chance for any more nights together. It was a small, invisible moment that she didn't even know I stole from her, but steal it I did. And it was the last time I saw her alive. I only saw her back because my tired, selfish heart avoided a friend when it should have given the gift of its own time and presence. I know better. And I have to live with that memory. Time is a gift that doesn't even belong to me, but it was gifted by God, who spoke hours and minutes into being the moment He set the sun and the moon in the sky.

I stood at her memorial service though, and I got to bear witness to the generous way she had spent her life. I got to hear from person after person about how she'd poured herself into each one of them. We laughed, cried, and sang our hearts out in memory of a woman who was quirky and beloved, and I loved her too. She wasn't perfect—and she knew I wasn't either—but now I get to carry her in my heart where she reminds me that giving people our time is an act of radical generosity. It's countercultural to refuse to utter those three words we say without even thinking, "I'm too busy." I don't want to be too busy. I don't want to be hung up on whether my house is presentable or not. I want to be available.

I want to be willing to be interrupted. Period.

Dietrich Bonhoeffer described it like this in his book, *Life Together:*

We must be ready to allow ourselves to be interrupted by God. God will be constantly crossing our paths and canceling our plans by sending us people with claims and petitions. We may pass them by, preoccupied with our more important tasks. ... It is a strange fact that Christians and even ministers frequently consider their work so important and urgent that they will allow nothing to disturb them. They think they are doing God a service in this, but actually they are disdaining God's "crooked yet straight path."[3]

FRIENDSHIP CHALLENGE

Let's get real honest together. Write down the names of specific people who felt like an interruption to your week. Let's flip that on its head and consider what God might actually be asking us to say to them or do with them. Maybe it's as simple as listening, taking a walk, doing a project, or sharing a movie night. Write down their names and ask God what He'd like you to do for them this week.

DAY 3

CRY AND CELEBRATE TOGETHER

So far, I'm hoping we've learned at least two things about friendship together: (1) God is your forever friend, and (2) Friendship welcomes interruptions. Along the way there really isn't room for worrying what your friends will think about the current state of your life, because true friends are more interested in the state of your heart than the state of your house. I love how The Message describes the incarnation—that sacred moment when God wrapped Himself up in human skin, feelings, body, and soul. John 1:14 says: "The Word became flesh and blood, and *moved into the neighborhood*" (emphasis mine). Jesus closed the gap between God and us by pulling up a chair alongside the daily lives of humanity so that we could know Him because He would make Himself known to us.

We are invited to do the same thing Jesus did: be willing to experience life with the community around us, giving our friends the same gift Jesus did—the gift of our presence—to show up and do one of two things.

READ ROMANS 12:15, AND WRITE DOWN WHAT THESE TWO THINGS ARE:

"_____ with those who _____; _____ with those who _____."

In other words, showing up for our friends can look as simple as doing the ugly cry with them or joining their celebrations with whooping and hollering and confetti. It sounds simple, but it takes discipline. It takes intentionality. And more often than we admit, it takes courage.

Jesus' example is so radical because He lived it. He lived out the whole arc of the human emotional spectrum—from weddings to funerals. He literally rejoiced as well as wept in public, and we have it recorded in Scripture. Two of what might be His most well-known miracles take place in these settings—at the joy of a wedding and in the despair of a death.

Read both stories, and write out in your own words what the atmosphere might have been like at each event:
John 2:1-11

John 11:17-36

According to John 11:3 how did Jesus feel about Lazarus?

How did Lazarus' sisters describe his relationship with Jesus?

The emotional energy at both events is off the charts—delight and despair, passion and gut-wrenching grief, hope and doubt. And Jesus willingly stepped into both environments and into the deep well of human emotions. I don't know about you, but sometimes I can be intimidated by the emotional highs and lows of my friends. It can be hard to know the right words to say in the midst of their grief or how to balance their celebration with my own insecurities. Those are the nitty gritty details behind the scenes of Romans 12:15, which is why I love getting a glimpse at the details surrounding Jesus' interactions with His friends in both their highs and their lows.

Bible commentaries allow us to paint a vivid picture of what those moments meant to the people living them. Behind the scenes of the story of the wedding in Cana we learn,

> A wedding is always a gala occasion, and in a village like Cana it would be a community celebration. "Refreshments" were provided for all guests. ... To fail in providing adequately for the guests would involve social disgrace. In the closely knit communities of Jesus' day, such an error would never be forgotten and would haunt the newly married couple all their lives. The situation prompted Mary's urgency when she informed Jesus of the emergency.[4]

Dancing, love, laughter, and passion. Seven days of joy, food, family, telling stories, and catching up on life and celebrating—and the vital importance of being able to provide generously for all your guests. And there was Jesus, right at the heart of it.

And a death? The desperate despair of loss. In the shortest verse in Scripture we know that "Jesus wept" (John 11:35). Commentaries paint for us the nuances so that we can see and experience the picture more vividly:

> The third word, ... ("wept"), means to shed tears quietly. It may be contrasted with the loud and ostentatious weeping ... of the hired mourners (v. 33), which was artificial. ... Jesus' sorrow impressed the onlookers with the depth of his concern.[5]

Are we brave enough to follow Jesus' example and open up our hearts to the raw emotions of our friends?

Describe a reaction you've had to someone else's scary sorrow.

Describe a reaction you've had to someone else's overpowering joy.

Recently, over hamburgers and corn on the cob, our pastor's wife told me how she's spent the last four years walking with a friend through the long, slow, terrible valley of grief. I was sort of stunned. Four years! Who has the guts to go that kind of distance? Who has it in them to commit to a friend through the terrible roller coaster of grief for that long? It's rare. It's holy. It's heroic. It's a gift.

After my mom died I had friends quit me because my grief was too heavy to carry. I don't blame them. There were many days I wished I could have quit it myself. Grief is exhausting, and if you have the choice, it's a luxury to choose to avoid it. But on an ordinary Monday afternoon, there was this woman of faith telling me how she knew from the get-go that she was going to commit to the whole journey through grief with her friend.

Because like all hard and painful things, the only way through is through. And if you have a friend willing to walk that dark road with you, you might have a decent chance of making it out on the other side. But even with a friend by your side, it will be hard to find the bits and pieces of yourself to put them back together again in a pattern you can recognize in the mirror.

The strange thing about joy is that it can have the same effect—sometimes it's too hard for our friends to embrace. Sometimes our joy pricks at the parts of their own lives where they're dissatisfied. Sometimes our joy highlights their hurts or losses. There are days when someone else's joy feels more like a threat than a celebration. The bizarre underbelly of joy taints when it should encourage, threatens when it should inspire, diminishes when it should enlarge.

Ask any woman struggling with infertility how she feels when she's invited to just one more baby shower. Ask any motherless daughter how Mother's Day feels. Ask any aspiring author what it's like to hear your friend's book hit the bestseller's list. Ask any coworker what it means when your friend makes the team, gets the opportunity, the raise, or the promotion that you didn't. You know what I'm talking about, right?

When was the last time you were so sad you felt like what your soul was experiencing was bigger than your body could contain? When was the last time your soul wept?

When was the last time you were so filled with delight and the desire to share your news and celebrate with someone that you couldn't possibly hold it all in? When was the last time your soul rejoiced?

The thing about Jesus is how through all of those experiences He is in the business of making all things new. Write out Revelation 21:5a (the first part of the verse):

God, in His infinite wisdom and His inability to be limited by sin, is constantly transforming our lives and our faith. Literally. In both stories we've studied above, Jesus used the experiences to transform. To make something new. To transform water into something much more special. To transform death into life. The wedding at Cana and the death of Lazarus bear witness to Jesus' transformative nature. In His kingdom nothing is wasted; no grief or joy is left to stand alone. Both are arrows pointing us back to the God who is constantly transforming us more and more into His own image.

If we will bravely enter into the joy and sorrow of our friends it will transform us and them because it will always point us back to Christ. Listen to how *The Expositor's Bible Commentary* describes the transformative nature of Jesus' first miracle that changed way more than the water:

> The purpose of Jesus' first miracle after entering Galilee is not stated. ... The nature of the miracle is very plain. Jesus had come to bring about conversion: water to wine, sinners to saints. And this latter miracle of transformation occurred in almost complete obscurity. Few know when or how it happened, but they know that it did happen.
>
> The effect of this miracle is noteworthy. It marked the beginning of a ministry accompanied by supernatural power; and it proved so convincing to the new disciples that they "put their faith in him." The deed helped confirm the conclusion they had drawn from their previous interviews with him: Jesus must be the Messiah.[6]

At a wedding, in a totally unexpected way, Jesus began His ministry of transformation—of making all things new—starting with the people around Him. The delightful quality of the miracle Jesus performed on the water wasn't about the pleasure it brought to the guests. It was about the change He was offering to bring about in their lives.

This is the same story we see unfold outside a tomb in Bethany:

> Why should [Jesus] be glad that he was not present to save Lazarus from death, or to comfort the sisters, and why should Lazarus's death bring any benefit to the disciples? Jesus considered this an opportunity for a supreme demonstration of power that would certify the Father's accreditation of him as the Son and confirm the faith of the sisters and the disciples. He was certain of the outcome.[7]

To make ourselves vulnerable to experience the grief and the joy of our friends is to make ourselves available to being changed—transformed—by the Christ who is always present on all our journeys on the emotional spectrum. When we let our fears, insecurities, or awkwardness stop us from fully entering into the experiences of the people around us, we limit the transformative impact the Holy Spirit can have on our lives. While we might not know how to put those experiences into words, He does. He's the friend available to process all of it with us.

Write out Romans 8:26.

That second half of the verse is translated in a variety of ways—all of them sweet with the tender intimacy of how closely God is willing to walk with us as we try to make sense of our sorrows and joys and the sorrows and joys of the people around us:

CSB: The Spirit himself intercedes for us with unspoken groanings.

NIV: The Spirit himself intercedes for us through wordless groans.

NLT: The Holy Spirit prays for us with groanings that cannot be expressed in words.

ESV: The Spirit himself intercedes for us with groanings too deep for words.

MSG: He does our praying in and for us, making prayer out of our wordless sighs, our aching groans.
ROMANS 8:26

In every translation we get the raw ability of the Holy Spirit to express even the things we can't manage to put into words ourselves. He is our constant, trustworthy companion as we try to make sense of our experiences and participate in the journeys of the people we love. I don't want to miss that chance. I don't want my own self-consciousness, selfishness, or tiredness to distract me from participating in the life-changing work of God in me and in the people around me.

But I know I have failed and I will fail again, and so I'm desperate to learn from Jesus' closest friends who stand as a cautionary tale for what not to do when someone we love is desperate for support.

READ MATTHEW 26:36-45, WHEN JESUS' CLOSEST FRIENDS UTTERLY MISSED THE CHANCE TO HELP HIM CARRY THE HEAVY LOAD OF HIS WORRY AND HIS GRIEF.

I've always thought the worst betrayal of the night was Peter's denial of Jesus, but the more I studied this passage, the more terrible this moment grew in my mind. In the moment when Peter denied Jesus we don't know if there was anything he could have actually said or done to bring comfort to Jesus, His dearest friend.

But in the garden, in the dark of night, Jesus spelled out exactly what His friends could do to encourage and comfort Him. And they failed Him 100 percent.

The sense of betrayal He must have felt at returning to find them fast asleep, not once, not twice, but three times (interestingly the same number of times Peter would deny Him verbally later that night) must have cut Him deeply before He even encountered Judas and the soldiers in the garden.

I'm desperate not to disappoint my Jesus. I'm desperate for His help in keeping watch with Him. I don't want to miss Him. I want to be awake with Him and for Him. But how you might ask? Well, we know that Jesus shows up in the faces and the stories and the voices, in the joys and sorrows of the people we encounter on what feels like totally ordinary Mondays, Tuesdays, or Sundays. He shows up in the lives of our whiny children, our difficult family members, and our struggling friends.

It's right there in black and white. If you want to comfort Jesus in His most suffocating sorrows or celebrate with Him in His most tremendous triumphs, you have to start with the people around you—the people Jesus has trusted to you, the men and women who bear His image.

FRIENDSHIP CHALLENGE

Let's start right here, right now. Make a list below of the people in your life who could use your company this week—whether they're walking a journey of joy or sorrow, excitement or despair. Write their names down and then make the time to connect with them this week. And wait and see how you're transformed by it—by meeting Jesus in the lives of the people around you.

It doesn't take much. And sure sometimes the showing up can make us feel awkward. It might make us feel embarrassed but only for the few minutes it takes us to stop thinking about ourselves. As soon as we're able to look past ourselves and focus on our friend, neighbor, or coworker, the sooner we're able to forget about saying the right thing and simply start saying the next thing.

You might be surprised how helpful that is to keep in mind. Just say the next thing—*pepperoni or cheese? Coffee or tea? Here, I knitted this for you. No need to return the pie dish. I picked up coloring books for the kids. Where's the laundry? I'm going to fold it while we watch a movie together.* Just keep showing up and saying the next thing and that kind of friendship will wrap itself around our friends' sorrows or joys simply by being willing to be present.

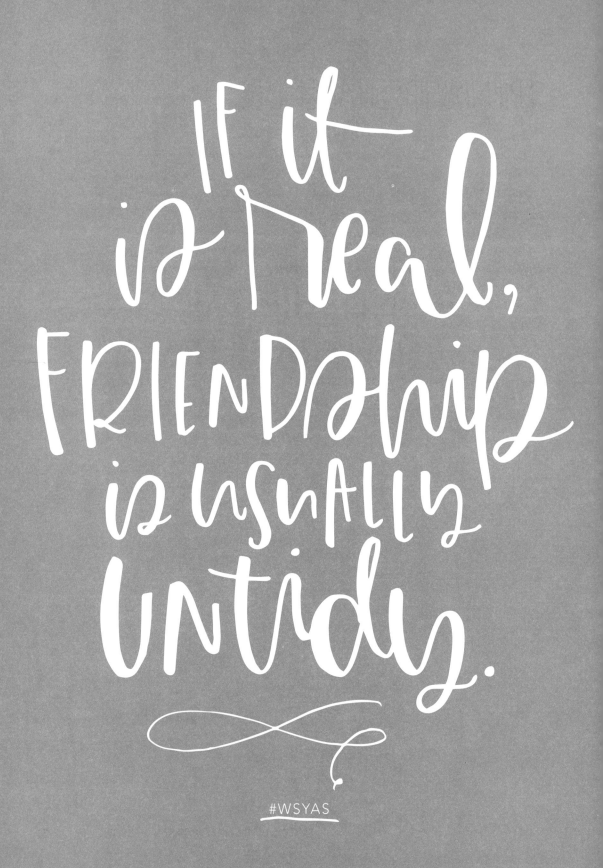

If it is real, FRIENDSHIP is usually untidy.

FRIENDSHIP TAKES VULNERABILITY

*Jesus said to her, "I am the resurrection and the life.
The one who believes in me, even if he dies, will live."*

JOHN 11:25

Friendship takes Vulnerability

VIEWER GUIDE: SESSION 2

Watch the Session 2 video and discuss with your group the following questions:

1. When you hear the word *vulnerability,* what memories of friendship (both good and bad) come to mind?

2. Why do you think vulnerability can feel so awkward?

3. Aliza told the story about processing her mother's cancer with her friend Sarah. Share an experience where the Lord has provided the right person for a certain season of your life.

4. How does self-sufficiency keep us from being vulnerable with others?

5. How have hurts in your past kept you from finding community and being vulnerable with other women in the present?

6. Alia talked about her friend that helped her through her depression. How has God surprised you by the friendships in your own life?

7. How have hurts within the community of the church skewed your perspective of friendship? What are you learning in this Bible study to help you overcome this perspective?

8. Aliza said, "Vulnerability is such a powerful tool toward healing." How have you seen evidence of this in your life?

9. Deidra posed the question, "What if my Sunday best really is my vulnerable self?" Think about this question. How does this question change the way we approach our relationships, especially in the context of the Christian community?

10. With your group, highlight any meaningful truths you took away from today's conversation at the table.

Video sessions available for purchase
at *LifeWay.com/WeSavedYouASeat*

GET HONEST WITH GOD

Friendship that requires us to open our front doors just the way we are and stop playing "fine" in front of our friends, that makes us make time and won't let us make small talk, can land us feeling emotionally naked and desperately vulnerable. Like you're standing on your best friend's front doorstep in your pajamas with bed head and ugly cry face left over from the night before, wondering if she's going to open the door. If she's going to be comfortable with this raw version of you. If she's going to invite you in or if she's going to make excuses to move you on out—especially if you didn't call first to let her know that you were coming over.

There's this terrifying moment between heartbeats when you don't know yet what she's going to say or how she's going to react. You're just standing there with all your raw honesty waiting for her to take her turn and respond. Waiting for her to stretch out an arm and wrap you up in her safe place or for the frown to leak across her face as she tries to make sense of this version of you, this version that clearly makes her uncomfortable.

In or out. What will it be? Your heart beats and waits and hopes and holds its breath.

Can you trust a friend with all your raw vulnerability, or should you have stopped to grab a brush and some concealer before showing up? Should you have stopped first to cover up and put yourself together?

Of course the temptation to cover up isn't just about how we look and whether we've cried our makeup off or not. It's about taking the risk to show up with our unairbrushed stories of marriage or motherhood or loss or singleness or homesickness or depression or failure. It's whether we can trust our friends to let us tell them how desperate we are to find ways to cope through the toddler years or the teenage years or the unemployed years, and will they still look at us the same when they hear how angry we can feel toward our own children, our roommates, our God? Will they still accept us if we crack into an awkward fit of weeping when we learn one more friend just got engaged and we're still single?

Where can we take all these vulnerable feelings if we can't take them to our friends? Can we come out of hiding and let ourselves be really seen? Can we just stand there in the middle of our lives and let our friends read right up to where we are and trust them with what comes next, even when we have no idea what that might be?

The thing is, trusting our friends is a reflection of how much we are willing to trust the God who created them. Until we can trust God with our naked vulnerability it will be impossible to trust other people. Do you? Do you trust God to be a friend who won't let you down, especially if you feel like God *has* let you down?

Can you trust God with your honest feelings? Can you trust Him with your whole vulnerable heart? With your disappointments? Go ahead, tell it like it is.

When have you felt like God has let you down?

It's such an awkward question, isn't it? But it's an honest one. If we can't bring our honest questions and fears that God will (or has) let us down to God Himself, the Author of all our relationships, then who can we ask? And here's the thing: We wouldn't be the first to ask that question. We wouldn't be the first to accuse God of letting us down. Mary and Martha already went there.

Those sisters were so comfortable in their friendship with Jesus, so sure of His love and acceptance, that they comfortably accused Him of letting their brother, Lazarus, die when they believed Jesus could have healed him.

That's huge. That's a wow kind of accusation. That's nuclear level friendship disappointment. But instead of stewing silently about it, Mary and Martha brought every ounce of their crushing hurt and sadness to Jesus Himself. They absolutely trusted He was the right place to go with that kind of disappointment. Their grief was raw and naked, and they didn't try to hide any of it from Him.

And Jesus?

He took it. He leaned in. He listened. He got it. And He stepped right into the chasm of their own terrible grief until it became His own. And more than that—He responded in uniquely individual ways to each of the sisters. These women were so much like each of us—straight-spoken, bold Martha, the doer, and reflective Mary, the listener.

Read John 11:20, and describe how each sister responded to hearing that Jesus had finally arrived in their town days after their beloved brother had died.

What did Martha do?

What did Mary do?

Martha was a woman of action, and that's where Jesus met her grief. She demanded action, and He assured her action was coming.

> Then Martha said to Jesus, "Lord, if you had been here, my brother wouldn't have died. Yet even now I know that whatever you ask from God, God will give you."
> JOHN 11:21-22

I love how Martha not-so-subtly continued to prod Jesus to *do* something already.

In verse 23 what action did Jesus assure her was coming?

And sweet, determined Martha, I can just imagine her heart sinking heavy into her chest as she said to her dear friend Jesus, "I know that he will rise again in the resurrection at the last day" (v. 24). That feels so far off, doesn't it? "The last day" is a long and terrible time to wait to be reunited. Any of us who've lost people know how terrible that kind of wait can feel.

But Jesus had an answer for Martha's action-hungry heart. Standing before her, the friend she was afraid might have disappointed her trust, proved Himself deeply faithful. He looked into her eyes that must have been bloodshot from crying and said to her with what I imagine must have been ineffable tenderness combined with unshakable assurance:

> I am the resurrection and the life. The one who believes in me, even if
> he dies, will live.
> JOHN 11:25

I mean! There He was, standing before her, the living answer to her crushing disappointment and desperate hunger for action. He is "the resurrection and the life." This friend Himself carries the answer within His holy, God-breathed DNA. He was God's response to her desperate desire for action in the face of death. Life runs in His veins and He offered it to Martha—and He offers it to you and me—and then He asked this haunting question:

Verse 26b: "Do _____ _____ this?"

Do we? Can we? Dare we take Him at His word?

Martha did. And being the wonderful woman of action that she was, she ran back to her sister Mary to tell her,

> The Teacher is here and is calling for you.
> JOHN 11:28

Then it was Mary's turn to bring her disappointed friendship to her friend, Jesus. To keep on being vulnerable even in the face of bruised trust.

In verses 29 and 31 the same adverb is used twice to describe how Mary went to Jesus. What is it?

She didn't hesitate to go to Jesus. She didn't hide or sulk; she went at once to the Friend who could make sense of what had happened to them. It had been four days since her brother died and her exhausted tears were still brimming over as she fell at Jesus' feet and repeated what her sister had already said,

> Lord, if you had been here, my brother would not have died!
> JOHN 10:32

That exclamation mark at the end of the sentence in my CSB Bible translation cuts deeply when I read it. It's the point of the knife digging into my heart, and I can imagine it felt the same to Jesus. Look at His reaction to Mary. No calm or rational conversation about what comes next. In response to this sister and her outpouring of emotion, we see Jesus mirror her grief with His own.

> When Jesus saw her crying, and the Jews who had come with her crying, he was deeply moved in his spirit and troubled.
> JOHN 11:33

Other versions translate the word "crying" as "weeping" (NIV). And it's not a quiet or polite kind of crying. No, it's the kind of loud, awkward, terrible, almost inhuman sound of grief that can terrify and embarrass listeners. The NIV Study Bible tells us, "Both times the word denotes a loud expression of grief, i.e., 'wailing.'"[1] Then with compassion and grief "Jesus wept" (v. 35).

Ours is a God we can vent to, ours is a God who will cry with us, but most crucial—ours is a God who will raise our deepest hurts from the dead because He is just as angry as we are at what sin steals from us. The Greek words used in John 11:33 for "deeply moved"—or *angry*—"probably indicates Jesus' anger against sin's tyranny and death."[2] And then our Jesus, our God who gets our human emotions of grief and disappointment from the inside out, from inside the very skin of humanity, proves Himself faithful and powerful enough to raise back to life what was once dead. Jesus raised Lazarus, who had been dead for days, by name—just like He will raise you and me. Just like He calls us by name. And what is required from us in order to see that glory of God in action?

> Jesus said to her, "Didn't I tell you that if you believed you would see the glory of God?"
> JOHN 11:40

We have to believe in order for Him to raise us and our dead and disappointed hearts from the tomb. Can we do it? Will we bring our broken hearts to Him? Will we trust and believe in Him so that we will hear His voice call us by name and raise back to life everything we thought had died in us and in our friendships? Dare we be that vulnerable with our God, our friend, and our Father? Maybe the better question is, how do we dare *not*?

FRIENDSHIP CHALLENGE

If vulnerability starts with Jesus, what do you need to tell Him today? What have you been holding back? Will you trust Him to mourn it with you and then to raise it back up from the dead?

On one side of a note card or index card or piece of paper, answer this sentence as honestly as you can:

Lord, if You had been here, my _____ wouldn't have died. (And remember, it doesn't have to be a person, it could be a dream, a hope, a project, a job, or a relationship—be as specific as you can.)

Let Him weep with you.

Now, let's trust Him to raise it from the dead.

On the other side of the card write down and then pray this prayer with Jesus: "Father, I thank You that You heard me. I know that You always hear me." Then write this sentence, maybe in all capitals, "I BELIEVE I WILL SEE THE GLORY OF GOD."

STOP TRYING TO BE IMPRESSIVE AND START BEING YOU

Once you believe that God loves you just the way you are, you can start to open your door and your life to let other people into the messy parts. This is the way we help our guests feel at home in our houses as well as in our lives. Then even our disappointments become appointments with the God who redeems all things. Can we become so secure in our vulnerability with Jesus that it spills over into trusting others with that same kind of vulnerability? Will we open our doors and our lives to the people around us who might also disappoint us? Let me rephrase that, to the people around us who will most certainly disappoint us at some point?

Maybe we're worried that if we let people see us or know us (how we really are) then we'll lose their admiration or respect. Worse yet, maybe we're afraid they'll unfollow us. Maybe that's why we're so attached to the picture of ourselves that we've constructed. After all we've been groomed by our culture to present a flawless version of ourselves to the people around us. We edit our homes and our Facebook pictures; our Instagram updates and filters reflect our Sunday best so that they communicate a version of ourselves that reflects the person we want to be. Yet, if we're honest, these things don't reflect the version of ourselves that we actually are.

So let's start there. Complete this sentence:

> I want people to think that I am _____ because I'm afraid they won't like me if they discover I am actually _____.

It's OK. We all have a version of ourselves we'd prefer instead of our actual reality. This is why I love Paul—the apostle with exceedingly grand qualifications who wasn't afraid to wave them around on the one hand but on the other hand was utterly unimpressed by his own bio. Come and see for yourself.

GO TO PHILIPPIANS 3:3-6 AND READ PAUL'S RÉSUMÉ.

Focusing on verses 5-6, write down Paul's seven most impressive résumé qualifications on the left side of the chart below. (We'll come back to the other side.)

PAUL'S CREDENTIALS	PAUL'S REALITY

Paul's life was the picture perfect appearance of godliness, holiness, and piety. It was the pinnacle of accomplishment in his time and culture, but Paul was utterly unimpressed by his own credentials because he had a ringside seat to the state of his own heart.

How did he describe himself in 1 Timothy 1:15?

Paul, never one to mince words, said he considered all his so-called accomplishments, "garbage, that I may gain Christ and be found in him, not having a righteousness of my own that comes from the law, but that which is through faith in Christ" (Phil. 3:8-9, NIV).

Paul painted a gripping picture for us of the truth that was first spoken to the prophet Samuel before he anointed a young, unheard of shepherd boy named David as the future king of Israel. When none of the seven strapping sons that were presented to Samuel were identified by God's Spirit as the future king, Samuel was stumped. And I love God's response in the language from the New King James translation:

> But the LORD said to Samuel, "Do not look at his appearance or at his physical stature, because I have refused him. **For *the* LORD *does* not *see* as man sees; for man looks at the outward appearance, but the** LORD **looks at the heart."**
> 1 SAMUEL 16:7, NKJV (EMPHASIS MINE)

We can crop and highlight and filter ourselves all we want, but the Holy Spirit sees through the sham with all-knowing eyes that penetrate into the core of our hearts. There is no filtering, no editing, and no hiding the truth of who we are from God. Paul knew this. And when it comes to stripping himself down to his bare bones under the gaze of the church in Corinth, who had become star struck by the so-called "super-apostles" of the day, Paul turned fame on its head when his only claims to it were a long grocery list of his failures.

> Go back to the chart we started on Paul. On the right hand side, fill in all the disasters and painful losses listed in 2 Corinthians 11:24-33 that characterized Paul's actual ministry. There are a lot of them, aren't there?

Rather than camouflaging his shame, his abuse, his crushing torture, Paul leaned into this weakness as the only safe place because:

> "[God's] power is perfected in weakness." Therefore, I will most gladly boast all the more about my weaknesses, so that Christ's power may reside in me. So I take pleasure in weaknesses, insults, hardships, persecutions, and in difficulties, for the sake of Christ. For when I am weak, then I am strong.
> 2 CORINTHIANS 12:9b-10

We live in a culture that's uncomfortable with weakness—one that would prefer to dress up even our weaknesses as strengths. But as Pastor Tim Keller wrote,

> Like Paul, we can say, "I don't care what you think. I don't even care what I think. I only care about what the Lord thinks."[3]

Can we say that? Are we willing to lean into that kind of self-forgetfulness? Because surely that's the only way to freedom, the only way to cut through the sticky web of personal promotion that spans the corridors of our lives, our TVs, our smartphones, and our tired minds.

I believe it's a choice with life and death consequences, because women are starving for more than status updates and 140 character connections. It's up to you and me to let them in so they can discover that they're not alone in their doubts, fears, and failures. So they can trust that we will be friends who are the same versions of ourselves, whether online or over a sink of dirty dishes.

People feel the most at home if you're willing to let them see you at your most real. Can we rethink the idea of our "Sunday best" together? As Deidra asked, *What if our Sunday best really is our most vulnerable self?* After all, those are the people invited to come to Him:

> Come to me, all of you who are weary and burdened, and I will give you rest.
> MATTHEW 11:28

> Come, everyone who is thirsty, come to the water; and you without silver, come, buy, and eat! Come, buy wine and milk without silver and without cost!
> ISAIAH 55:1

It's the parched, those with chapped lips and souls, and the starving who can't hide their hunger who are invited to come—just as they are—for their needs to be met by the Christ who came to meet us at the crossroads of our desperate need and His abundant provision. But to receive we have to be willing to admit our own unedited, unfiltered needs.

When last did you feel close or comfortable with someone because of how impressive they were? Isn't it the people who let us see them at their crushed cereal underfoot, everyday ordinary that make us feel the most at home? Because we can exhale and let down our own attempts to impress and let our real, vulnerable selves out into the open. Much like changing out of those too-tight skinny jeans and exhaling into a pair of sweatpants, surely we can also do this with our friendships if we want them to fit us; if we want to fit them.

FRIENDSHIP CHALLENGE

Complete this sentence and then choose at least one person to put it into practice with this week.

I want to offer _____ to the women around me, so
I'm going to have to _____.

Here, I'll go first: I want to offer **an assurance that what they're doing between the diapers and the dishes is significant kingdom work** to the women around me, so I'm going to have to **let them see my life right there in the middle of those things—even on the days it feels messy or uncool—if I want to reflect God's view of the extraordinary right there in the middle of the ordinary.**

DARE TO STAY WHEN THE GOING GETS TOUGH

If anyone modeled what vulnerability looks like, it has to be Jesus. Leaving behind the security of heaven, of His title, His throne, His position, He let Himself be delivered naked into the world of poverty and constant misunderstanding and humiliation. In an age when Caesars were claiming they were descended from the gods, the God of the universe sent His only Son into the world under the cover of almost total obscurity.

Caesar Augustus decreed that all people in his kingdom should be registered in their hometowns. Augustus was known as Gaius Octavius or Octavian until about 27 BC. The Roman senate actually gave him the name Augustus, meaning honored, dignified, and giving him the status of a god.[4] While Augustus accomplished many great things for his kingdom and established many policies that contributed to a greater peace and stability throughout the Roman Empire, his rule and his peace would not compare to that of the King born into humble circumstances in Bethlehem.[5]

Luke's Gospel is the account of two kings who promised salvation—one earthly king who has long passed, and King Jesus, who continues to offer His salvation from the cross to all.

The tension and choice that existed then are still true for us today—which king will we choose to serve, to follow, and to believe? Because friendship with Jesus promises the exact opposite of comfort, luxury, or position—the promises that our culture advertises. Instead, friendship with Jesus is a lifelong lesson in vulnerability. The kind that hurts. The kind that teaches us to stoop lower, to serve longer, to lean into brokenness instead of trying to avoid it. The closer our friendship with Jesus grows the more we will feel the weight of the cross that He has asked us to carry alongside Him cutting into our shoulders.

Then Jesus said to his disciples, "If anyone wants to follow after me, let him deny himself, take up his cross, and follow me."
MATTHEW 16:24

The kind of vulnerability that Christ asks of us might literally cost us our lives. It will certainly cost us our egos, our self-centered plans, our determination to get our own way and to control our own image management. Jesus constantly exposes what's really going on in our greedy, self-involved hearts because He is not fooled by the layers of words and pixels we try to use to disguise our true motives.

And we're not the first to have to face that unmasking.

After Jesus fed the five thousand, the crowds continued to follow Him, but He was quick to point out their motivation. John's Gospel describes why He had suddenly acquired so many new disciples:

Jesus answered, "Truly I tell you, you are looking for me, not because you saw the signs, but because you ate the loaves and were filled."
JOHN 6:26

They couldn't think beyond their own bellies; they were following Him for the free food He had provided only a few paragraphs earlier! But Jesus was offering them Himself. "I am the bread of life" (v. 35), He told them.

READ JOHN 6:35 AND FILL IN THE BLANKS OF WHAT JESUS PROMISES US.

"No one who comes to me will ever be _____, and no one who believes in me will ever be _____ again" (John 6:35).

God, Himself, is always the answer to what we need—whether it's food or life. Like He would later offer Himself to Mary and Martha as the resurrection and the life, He now offers Himself as the living bread to the people who've been following Him since He fed five thousand of them. Whereas the bread He'd multiplied for them and the manna that had come down from heaven to feed their ancestors wouldn't be able to defeat the inevitability of hunger and death, Jesus promises that people who are willing to eat the bread of life He is offering in Himself will live forever.

But that kind of relationship, that kind of trust, it's uncomfortable. It's not instantly gratifying. It requires investing parts of ourselves instead of simply stuffing and numbing ourselves. It requires taking what Jesus offers and digesting it until it becomes part of who we are, from the inside out. And the people were quick to point that out:

> "This teaching is hard. Who can accept it?" ... From that moment many of his disciples turned back and no longer accompanied him.
> JOHN 6:60,66

They quit Jesus and His uncomfortable teachings that want to get up in our business and change us from the inside out instead of just satisfying our cravings. But then came Jesus' question to His twelve remaining disciples that rings full and rich with its own human vulnerability along with a holy challenge:

> So Jesus said to the Twelve, "You don't want to go away too, do you?"
> JOHN 6:67

It's even more haunting in the NLT version of the Bible: "Are you also going to leave?"

I can hear the desperate vulnerability of a man who might lose His friends, but we mustn't miss also hearing the challenge from the God who doesn't want to lose our souls. It's twofold:

> (1) He is testing who we take our identity from. Who do we listen to?

> (2) He is testing the condition of our hearts. What do we want?

Listen to how those questions are unpacked by the *IVP New Testament Commentary*:

> The question they raise reveals their real problem: *This is a hard teaching. Who can accept it?* (v. 60). This is a profound question that points to their own hearts. By saying *Who can accept it?* they suggest they are not to blame, that this is too much for anyone to accept. But in fact it shows that they are not humbly docile, as true disciples in this Gospel are. A mark of docility is the ability and willingness to listen and receive. In this Gospel one's identity is known by whom one can and does listen to.[6]

In other words, your identity is who you can and will listen to. When you refuse to listen or say it's too hard to listen to Jesus, you're refusing to draw your identity from Jesus.

Again, let's go deeper with the commentary:

> God knows the condition of our hearts and sends circumstances that will reveal our hearts to us. How do we respond to such exposure? Does it drive us to despair or to deeper dependency upon the Lord?
>
> So Jesus issues another challenging question, this time to the Twelve: **You do not want to leave too, do you?** (v. 67). This question tests the heart, like the earlier one did (v. 61). ... They must make a choice then and there. Since Jesus knows people's interior dispositions (v. 64; cf. 2:25), he would know of their faith, so his question tests their hearts and reveals their response to themselves and to one another.[7]

In other words, what do they really want—food or faith? Sustenance or Jesus? Same goes for us. When our hearts are hurting, what do we really want? To numb the pain or to trust that it is being used in our lives by a good God whom we can trust?

How did Peter answer in John 6:68-69? Write it in your own words as if you were answering Jesus' question.

With honesty, Peter puts into words my own lonely heart: Where else would I possibly go? Who else would I possibly believe? Despite my doubts and the days I wish I could keep hiding or pretending, who else promises bread that transcends life and life that can't be smothered in the various graves that call my name—fear, doubt, insecurity, anxiety, worry, envy, and panic?

No, I'm with Peter. There's nowhere else trustworthy to go. If the choice is hiding my vulnerability in food or perfectly-curated images of my life on Instagram or pretending I'm the version of me that I think everyone expects versus handing my entire vulnerable self over to Jesus to cover me, welcome me, and name me as His own, I choose Jesus.

FRIENDSHIP CHALLENGE

Can you identify at least one area in your life where you've come to rely on instant gratification to numb out your hungers instead of facing your own vulnerabilities?

Now identify one practical action you're going to take this week to replace that numbing behavior with the bread of life from Jesus.

We can either ENCOURAGE -or- Compare. We can't do both.

FRIENDSHIP TAKES ENCOURAGEMENT

Adopt the same attitude as that of Christ Jesus.

PHILIPPIANS 2:5

FRIENDSHIP takes enCouragement

VIEWER GUIDE: SESSION 3

Watch the Session 3 video and discuss with your group the following questions:

1. How have you seen FOMO (the fear of missing out) affect your relationships?

2. How have you seen comparison damage relationships? How has comparison affected your own friendships?

3. Lisa-Jo noted that "The kingdom of God is a co-op, not a competition." How have you seen competition damage relationships within the community of believers?

4. Share personal examples of how encouraging others not only lifts up the one being encouraged but the one doing the encouraging as well.

5. How has social media helped or hurt your friendships?

6. Read Philippians 2:5-8. What should our attitudes be when we begin to feel the "roar of our own sense of entitlement"?

7. How can we intentionally choose to encourage our friends?

8. With your group, highlight any meaningful truths you took away from today's conversation at the table.

Video sessions available for purchase
at *LifeWay.com/WeSavedYouASeat*

ASK GOD FOR A HEART TRANSPLANT

OK, I'll be frank with you. This week might sting a bit. Because jealousy is not a fun topic to talk about. And because of all the insidious ways a friendship can disintegrate, comparison must be one of the worst. It dishonors the gift of vulnerability that we know from last week is essential for a friendship to flourish. But we're going to go there. We need to go there. Because we don't want the thing your friend is the most excited to share with you to become the thing she wishes she could hide to prevent your jealousy. And on the other hand, we don't want you to unintentionally poke the bear of jealousy in your friends.

It feels like such an embarrassing admission, doesn't it, that we fall down the rabbit hole of comparing ourselves to other people? But it can pull you in and drain the life out of you before you even realize it's happening. And it doesn't seem to have any age limit—we're never too young or too old to get dragged into the sinking sand of comparison.

We live in a world where in unexpected seconds we can stumble into comparison when only moments earlier we were filled up with the contentment of our own lives. Just last weekend I stood at the door of our living room watching my people play across the floor. There were piles of laundry and undone dishes. There were blocks and tiny dolls and all the miniature clothes to go with them. It was a mess, and it filled me up with a kind of sticky, delicious happiness. All these people were mine to call "home," mine to love, mine to do life with in this house tucked behind a row of pine trees.

I was so full of the kind of love that surprises us on the best kind of ordinary days that I couldn't move. I just stood in awe, watching the wonder of my life play out before my eyes. The kind of wonder I never could have explained to my teenage self who was so set on being cool and fitting in. The kind of wonder that comes from seeing enough of the broken parts of life to recognize the moments that are highlighted by the tender light of everyday miracles. I took a photo so I could remember it and then turned back down the hall to our bedroom because the ultimate miracle was that my family had sent me to enjoy a Saturday afternoon nap.

As I climbed into bed, I reached for my phone to set an alarm. But then I made the mistake of opening Instagram. And right before my very eyes I watched my little cocoon of contentment explode into a million pieces of discontent. I scrolled through photo after photo of women who'd been invited to a retreat I didn't even know about, authors who were writing profound words while I had my hair in a dirty ponytail and was still wearing my pajamas. Just like that, the comparison shattered all my satisfaction into miserable shards of envy. It literally took seconds. In one breath I was as fulfilled by my life as I'd ever been, and the next breath I gasped out the miserable grumblings of a toddler who sits surrounded by piles of presents, obsessed over the one thing she didn't get.

Victims of comparison attacks litter the Internet, our women's groups, our book clubs, Facebook updates, churches, and circles of friends. We live in a world where there are virtual warehouses of new ways we can find to covet our neighbor's house, family, and life. Nothing is as terrifying as thinking you don't matter because you can't do it like her.

In the space below, write down your own unexpected comparison moment. What were some of the feelings stirred within you?

One of the best ways to neutralize our effectiveness in the kingdom of God is for us to be tricked into thinking that we don't count. To give up, to sit down, to call it quits, to cry on frustrating afternoons that if we can't do it just like her then it's not worth doing it at all. Because, in the words of Priscilla Shirer, the enemy would "rather conspire to keep you in a constant state of mourning, grieving over who you *wish* you were, instead of relishing who you really *are*, exacerbated by insecurity and crippled by self-doubt."[1]

No wonder that this desperate, self-centered desire is at the root of every single other sin. Christian philosopher Francis Schaeffer said:

Every one of the Ten Commandments can be summed up in the last: "You shall not covet" (Ex. 20:17). ... Any time that we break one of the other commandments of God, it means that we have already broken this commandment, in coveting.[2]

Ouch. That's a hard one to hear. Are you brave enough to join me in recognizing the places in our lives where the enemy is lying to us? Where he's trying to convince us that if we aren't like her then we don't count?

Let's take a deep breath and write down a few of those tender spots. The places where we worry we don't count because we have felt counted out.

Think about the last week or the last month. Who have you compared yourself to and why? Start there so you can begin to unmask the lies that you've been sold. Fill in these blanks. You don't need to use names; you can just describe who it is you ache to be like. For example, moms who get to stay home, friends who can write full time for a living, women at church who are asked to serve in ways you haven't been, or the woman in the office next door who got that promotion.

I've been comparing myself to _____ because:

I'm often surprised by how easily I believe the thoughts that flutter through my head— how I treat them like gospel. But the true Scriptures tell us that,

The heart is more deceitful than anything else, and incurable—who can understand it?
JEREMIAH 17:9

Ouch again. When last did you question your own heart? Your motives for the comparison or jealousy you're feeling? When last did you pry into what's behind those feelings to get to the root of where they're coming from?

Take a moment to rewrite that sentence from Jeremiah 17:9. Put it into your own words. Words that speak to you. Words that will really get your attention. Only you know how to best force yourself to look into the truth about your own heart. Write your own version here:

Here's my attempt: *My heart is a big fat greedy liar that wants all the things everyone else has. Whether they're a good fit for me or not. Whether I even have the time for them or not. It's literally impossible for me to fix that myself. I need help. Who can help me?*

It's painful to admit, but there really is no one better at lying to ourselves than ourselves. How many times have we opened Facebook or Instagram only to catch a glimpse of an event we weren't invited to and resented the women in the picture? How many times have we secretly been disappointed by the good news of others? How many times have we gone home and cried frustrated tears that we weren't the one chosen, promoted, published, featured, voted in, engaged, or pregnant?

How many times have we translated those images into the assumption that the failure to connect or invite or include was because we were somehow found lacking? How often have we jumped from a photograph in a Facebook stream to a full-page story in our own heads that stars us as the excluded, overlooked, underappreciated victim? It's a dangerous role to play. Just listen to how Scripture describes the effect that kind of envy has on our hearts:

> But if you have bitter envy and selfish ambition in your heart, don't boast and deny the truth. Such wisdom does not come down from above but is earthly, unspiritual, demonic. For where there is envy and selfish ambition, there is disorder and every evil practice.
> JAMES 3:14-16

Isn't it interesting that James knows how experienced we are in the fine art of self-deception, making it almost impossible for us to recognize our own envy and selfish ambition? We pretend; we deny the truth. We go about our business and our carpool and our classes, and it becomes almost an unconscious decision to avoid that friend we're jealous of when she calls, texts, or to scroll past her Facebook statuses without leaving a comment.

That's the noose of comparison and envy tightening around your neck without you even realizing it. It's hard to swallow past that lump of dissatisfaction that grows bigger and bigger every time you think about that friend and how "unfair" it is that she has what you want. We might be shocked if someone actually read our thoughts out loud because we're so good at pretending we're not really thinking them, not really feeling all that terrible anger toward the person who has what we think should be ours.

Go back and reread how James described this kind of behavior, this so-called "wisdom." What are the three words he used to describe it in the verse quoted above (v. 15):

"Such wisdom does not come down from above but is _____,

_____, _____."

Where that kind of envy and selfish ambition exists, James says in words that should send chills down our spines: "there is _____ and every

_____ _____."

I don't know about you but those verses terrify me, because I'm so casual with my comparison. It's so normal to make a hundred different comparisons a day—to other women's homes, kids, teaching skills, recipes, meal planning, furniture, paint choices, opportunities, messy buns, eyeliner, or the way they wear their skinny jeans. It only takes one of these sinking deep enough into my definition of how I see myself for it to get a grip on my heart and start to poison my mind and our friendship.

And once the lie bites, the slow trickle of poison begins to build up over time in our veins—a steady drip of toxic comparison that poisons friendships:

Envy leads not only to foolish decisions, but it blocks the ability to weep with those who weep and rejoice with those who rejoice.[3]

It's impossible to compare *and* encourage. We can either love or compete. We can either empathize or resent. We can either celebrate or sulk. We can't do both.

But there is hope. God is a heart-knower, and He can liberate us from our hearts poisoned by the enemy's lies.

I the LORD search the heart and examine the mind.
JEREMIAH 17:10, NIV

The Great Physician, the Great Healer, the Tender Counselor has the antidote to the lies we believe if we'll only let Him treat us. David—the shepherd, the youngest of seven sons, the man who spent almost half of his life running away from jealousy that was trying to kill him—said, "you delight in truth in the inward being, and you teach me wisdom in the secret heart" (Ps. 51:6, ESV). Jesus, "the way, the truth, and the life" (John 14:6), is the only One who can open up your secret heart and gently extract the fangs of poison that are lodged there. The only One who can decapitate the lie wrapped tight around our poor, gasping hearts. He has promised that He will and we can hold Him to it. Here is the rescue verse, the verse we can cling to like a life preserver on the days we're drowning in our own jealousy:

I will give you a new heart and put a new spirit within you; I will remove your heart of stone and give you a heart of flesh.
EZEKIEL 36:26

Let's do what we did earlier and put this beautiful verse into our own words, so that we really hear the hope that it promises.

Paraphrase Ezekiel 36:26 with words that shout hope in your own voice so that you're more likely to really believe it.

Here's my version: *I will give you a heart that hasn't been soaked in the poison of comparison. I will put a fresh wind, a new spirit, a life-giving delight right into the very center of who you are. I will rescue you from your heart of stone—the heart that wants to drag you down to the bottom of the ocean and drown you in jealousy. And I will give you a fresh heart beating with the knowledge and wisdom of the Lord—one that beats so hard with God's love for your neighbors you'll feel it pounding through every part of your soul and every ordinary conversation.*

Jesus is the only One who can give us hearts of truth, hearts of flesh, hearts that aren't poisoned beyond recognition by the lie that we deserve what that other woman has and hearts that He calls by name that believe they are seen.

Jesus offers us a new heart if we are willing to receive Him as Savior and Lord. He will give us all of Himself to give us life, a desperate and daring rescue.

Tim Keller teaches that what we put in our "hallowed place" is what will define us. He said, "By giving God the praise He deserves, we will heal our worldview as well as our souls."[4] In other words, if we want our new hearts to survive the transplant, we have got to demote out of our hallowed places our obsession with others and what they've got versus what we think we deserve. We must silence "the roar of [our] own sense of entitlement."[5] We have to get our obsession with comparison to others *out* of the hallowed place—stop worshiping at the altar of self when we were built to worship at the altar of the only living God.

And then as the new heart does its work, pumping life and truth through us, hurt from exclusion and comparison will be drowned out by a new message:

> But the fruit of the Spirit is love, joy, peace, patience, kindness, goodness, faithfulness, gentleness, and self-control. The law is not against such things. Now those who belong to Christ Jesus have crucified the flesh with its passions and desires. If we live by the Spirit, let us also keep in step with the Spirit. Let us not become conceited, provoking one another, envying one another.
> GALATIANS 5:22-26

FRIENDSHIP CHALLENGE

It's time to uproot those lies that are trying to strangle our hearts, friends. Let's make two lists. First, go ahead and list all the things you've been jealous of that God has given to others. Now, one by one, cross them out. This is the drumbeat of our new Jesus-hearts. This is how we become set free.

WRITE OVER OR ABOVE OR NEXT TO THEM EACH OF THE FRUIT OF THE SPIRIT FROM GALATIANS 5:22-26.

WHAT GOD HAS GIVEN TO OTHERS	THE FRUIT OF THE SPIRIT

BEWARE! COMPARISON WILL KILL YOU EVERY TIME.

A few years back I was at a conference standing around chatting with several women—old friends and new—and we got to talking about friendship. About walking the difficult line of cheering for our sisters while secretly craving their success. Many of the women turned to me and exclaimed how good I am at this encouragement thing. Like it comes naturally. Like maybe it's easier for me. And I was stunned.

If only they could see inside my head. If only they could tune into my internal monologue. If only they knew about my late nights trying to talk myself off the ledge of thinking myself a worthless waste of time because I didn't do it like her, accomplish it in the same amount of time as them, or get recognized by that group.

There is a dark thing that hides at the fringes of my faith. I can feel it there. Lurking in the shadows. Waiting.

WAITING for the unkind word from someone I work with, church with, or raise children with.

WAITING for a 90-degree commute stuck in bumper-to-bumper gridlock in the ancient car with no air conditioning while pretty SUVs whip by me.

WAITING for the blog that is prettier, bigger, or more beloved than mine to catch my attention.

WAITING for the mom who is more organized, more disciplined, more engaged than I am.

WAITING for the house that is cleaner, bigger, more HGTV than mine.

WAITING for the job, the opportunity, the invitation that is more glamorous, more desirable, more interesting than my current one right now.

And in that moment, I feel it slink out of the shadows and onto my shoulder. Gently it strokes my hair, caresses my neck, and begins to whisper in my ear.

It whispers, "Unfair. Poor you. You *deserve* more." It understands me. It pets me. It tells me, "You *should* be angry. It's your *right* to feel frustrated. They don't know how *hard* you have it."

It offers me the opportunity to rant and sulk and feel justified in doing so. More often than I care to admit, I have allowed the dark thing to cover my mouth with a hard, hot hand and speak petty words on my mute behalf. It is never pretty. And it is not even original.

This is a lie that has been trying to strangle us since the beginning of time. Since Eve believed that she deserved to, "be like God, knowing good and evil" (Gen. 3:5). This— wanting to be like God, having all that He has—is the essence of entitlement. And we see it woven through the stories of Scripture, none so clearly as in the dysfunctional relationship between King Saul and the up and coming sheep herder and soldier, David. Their twisted and complicated relationship is a 3D example of how comparison and jealousy can literally kill any chance of trust or friendship, no matter how strong the relationship started out.

Take a look at some key events of Saul and David's relationship.

- Saul was impressed with the brave, young shepherd who was willing to fight the giant Goliath (1 Sam. 17).

- Saul offered David his own armor (1 Sam. 17:38-39).

- David defeated Goliath and Saul took David into his household (1 Sam. 17:50–18:2).

- David "was successful in everything Saul sent him to do" (1 Sam. 18:5).

- Saul put David in command of many of his soldiers. This pleased everyone (1 Sam. 18:5).

- GAME CHANGER: The women sang to celebrate the heroes as they returned: "Saul has killed his thousands, but David his tens of thousands" (1 Sam. 18:7).

- Saul's anger exploded. He became furious and resented the song and David. He complained that the people liked David more than him. His jealousy became terminal (1 Sam. 18:8-16).

- Saul had begun the pattern that would continue for several decades of trying to kill David and then feeling bad about it, only to have his jealousy boil over again until it became his defining character trait (1 Sam. 18–31).

- Saul was never able to kick the jealousy habit (1 Sam. 18–31).

Maybe you, like me, have grown up with the story of these two men since we watched it unfold on our coloring pages in Sunday School. Maybe we're too comfortable with it. Maybe we need a refresher that this terrible tale of the crippling effects of jealousy tore apart two friends and nearly an entire kingdom. Saul was utterly obsessed and utterly crippled by his jealousy. In the words of Drs. Cloud and Townsend in their book, *Safe People,* in Satan's kingdom we are tempted by our envy—our discontentment:

All of us are tainted with envy. Envy is intimately connected with coveting, and is best defined as a tendency to hate other people for having what we want. Envy says, "What is inside me is bad. What is outside me is good. I hate anyone who has something I desire."[6]

Saul's hatred for David was legendary.

> Let's count the number of times Saul tried to kill David. Skim through 1 Samuel 18–20; 23, and 26 to get a rough headcount of how many times Saul came close to killing David: _____

That kind of behavior sounds extreme, doesn't it? That sounds a million miles away from our modern, ordinary Thursday lives where we know how to be polite and how to congratulate people and often don't recognize the quiet resentment building in our souls toward other people. But this hatred that grows out of the seed of jealousy grows in the dark places of our hearts just like it did all throughout the Old Testament. This kind of hate is why Cain killed Abel (who got the recognition for a sacrifice that Cain thought he deserved; see Gen. 4), why Joseph's brothers wanted him dead because they hated that their father loved him best, why Rachel resented Leah for the children she so easily conceived (see Gen. 30:1-24), and why they both dragged their servant girls into their bitter feuding over who had more kids, more affection, and more status.

We are fools if we think that we don't share the murderous DNA of our spiritual ancestors. Let's read Matthew 5:21-22. Write out verse 22.

According to Jesus what makes us all murderers at heart?

And so even in our polite world today without a single confrontation, without raised voices or even a conscious acknowledgment of what's happening, a friendship can be decimated by the simple build up of a toxic and insurmountable wall of jealousy that is deadly. Every time our friend tries to reach out or connect, she smacks into the invisible wall we've built between her opportunity and our jealousy. After a while, she stops trying. And then we get to be angry with her all over again for abandoning us.

This is the terrible, destructive power of what envy breeds. Drs. Cloud and Townsend explain:

Envy makes us resent people who have something we don't have. It feeds on itself and is ultimately self-destructive. When we envy, the very people who are loving, safe, and generous become the bad guys in our eyes.[7]

Instead of becoming his greatest ally and most trusted general, David became Saul's obsession and threat. And a thousand years later David's most famous descendant, Jesus, would walk in His ancestor's footsteps with the jealousy of others dogging His every step.

The Spirit of the Lord is on me,
because he has anointed me
to preach good news to the poor.
He has sent me
to proclaim release to the captives
and recovery of sight to the blind,
to set free the oppressed.
LUKE 4:18

What had Jesus been sent to do?

But part of that freedom came at the cost of control to the ruling religious elite. At the time they ruled with prestige, iron fists, and crushing consequences for anyone who couldn't live up to the letter of the law. And Jesus called them on it. Jesus upset their balance of power with His new kingdom that promised freedom from the stranglehold the Pharisees had made of the law and its impossible-to-live-up-to standards.

> Then Jesus spoke to the crowds and to his disciples: "The scribes and the Pharisees are seated in the chair of Moses. Therefore do whatever they tell you, and observe it. But don't do what they do, because they don't practice what they teach. **They tie up heavy loads that are hard to carry and put them on people's shoulders, but they themselves aren't willing to lift a finger to move them.** They do everything to be seen by others: They enlarge their phylacteries and lengthen their tassels. They love the place of honor at banquets, the front seats in the synagogues, greetings in the marketplaces, and to be called 'Rabbi' by people.
>
> "But you are not to be called 'Rabbi,' because you have one Teacher, and you are all brothers and sisters. Do not call anyone on earth your father, because you have one Father, who is in heaven. You are not to be called instructors either, because you have one Instructor, the Messiah. The greatest among you will be your servant. Whoever exalts himself will be humbled, and whoever humbles himself will be exalted.
>
> "Woe to you, scribes and Pharisees, hypocrites! You shut the door of the kingdom of heaven in people's faces. For you don't go in, and you don't allow those entering to go in."
> MATTHEW 23:1-13 (EMPHASIS MINE)

The envy and rage of the Pharisees boiled over because Jesus was taking from them their status, their respect, and their followers:

> If we let him go on like this, everyone will believe in him, and the Romans will come and take away both our place and our nation.
> JOHN 11:48

Where did their jealousy take them? What was the response of the Pharisees according to Matthew 12:14; 26:4; Mark 14:1; Luke 22:2; and John 11:53?

In a bizarre twist of fate, who actually recognized the true motivation lurking behind the Pharisees' plot to kill Jesus for what it was—blinding jealousy? Read Mark 15:6-10 to identify that character.

What a deep shame I feel when I realize I've walked in those same footsteps, obsessed over those same thoughts, believed those same lies about entitlement, and stewed in those same fears that I'm going to lose out. Instead of being women who might mentor us, encourage us, or raise us up, envy turns friends into enemies and sisters into strangers. **Our only hope is the God who might have been killed at the hands of envy but was never subject to it.** Joe Rigney, assistant professor of theology and literature at Bethlehem College and Seminary, writes:

Christ died at the hands of envious men that he might deliver men from the same envy that nailed him to the cross. The jealous and malicious, the resentful and bitter, the covetous and the entitled—all of us have hope this Holy Week, because the One delivered up by our envy was raised up by the good pleasure of his Father.[8]

FRIENDSHIP CHALLENGE

PART 1: Friends, it's time to confess. It's time to get on our faces before God and tell Him how sorry we are for how we've been jealous of His daughters. It's time to honestly admit that we were wrong for wanting what He'd given to them. It's time to say sorry—to say sorry to God and, in our hearts, to say sorry to the women we've hurt by our jealousy.

Write that prayer here.

_____

_____

_____

_____

_____

_____

_____

_____

_____

_____

_____

PART 2: Now a quick word of warning about confessing jealousy beyond prayer and to another person. While it is sometimes healthy to confess our sins to the person we've wronged, sometimes it's a case of making ourselves feel better at the expense of making our friends feel worse. This seems to me especially true in the case of jealousy. Confessing jealousy to the person you're jealous of leaves that person in a very uncomfortable spot because there's nothing she can do about it, except maybe start to feel bad and horribly self-conscious. She can't unmake her gifts and opportunities, and we shouldn't expect her to. Confessing our jealousy puts the burden on her instead of where it should be—on us. It unfairly shifts the responsibility to process jealousy in a healthy way from the person in the know to the person who has no clue what's been going on.

So, if we want to bring jealousy out into the light so that the dark creature eating up our hearts can't continue to whisper its viscous, strangling lies to us anymore, what we need is a safe friend who's a neutral third party. Confession can be the key to unlock that dark room we pretend doesn't exist. But let's makes sure that we process the lie that says, "I don't matter if I don't have what she has" with someone who can't be hurt by that confession.

That kind of holy, hard conversation doesn't take the friend you've been jealous of hostage. Instead, that kind of conversation with a neutral third party can set you free. And it gives your friend a gift she'll never even know about—the gift of continuing to walk confidently in her calling without doubting herself and without being afraid of how it will impact her friendship with you. If you believe you need to confess your jealousy out loud, then ask God to help you find that third party friend who can walk you through that tender process.

PART 3: Finally, a note about guarding our friends against jealousy. There is a time to share our opportunities, accomplishments, and joys. But there's also a time to treasure them in our hearts, content with private delight. This is becoming harder and harder in a culture that glorifies sharing every tiny detail of our lives, but we can do better. We can remember to guard the hearts of our friends and find tender ways to share news that we know might cause damage to a friend whom we love. Surely the friendship is more significant than the news we're dying to share. Let's keep living Christ's challenge to die to ourselves, even in our moments of deepest accomplishment and grandest success. Let's die to the temptation to flash our news around like giddy children who don't know any better.

We do know better. And if we love our friends deeply, then we'll be deeply concerned with their well-being, and we'll handle our news and their hearts with extra care and consideration. Let's constantly be on the lookout for ways to guard our friendships. And sometimes that starts with what comes out of our own mouths or Instagram streams. Let's take the extra time and care when we're sharing news that we know has the potential to sow comparison and jealousy into a friendship that we hold dear. Let's care more about our friends than our own accomplishments. Let's tread carefully when treading on what we know are the hopes and dreams of the people we hold most dear.

BELIEVE ENCOURAGEMENT WILL SET YOU FREE

If our goal is healthy, whole hearts, then we need to be ruthless in rooting out our jealousy. In my experience, simply wishing jealousy away doesn't work. We need to replace it with something substantial, powerful, and life-giving. I believe that the antidote to jealousy is a combination of gratitude and encouragement—gratitude for what God has given you and the work He's doing in and through you and encouragement for the work He's doing in and through the lives around you. Choosing to encourage instead of compare is a powerful defensive play. But it doesn't always come easy. It is hard, deliberate work for every single one of us. So let's get to it.

Comparison is exhausting and self-destructive. The cycle is vicious and viciously effective. And it relies on a lie—the myth of scarcity. Because in Satan's kingdom, where we each want to be our own gods, there is no room for sharing, there is never enough to go around, and everything must be grabbed and hoarded to make sure we survive.

God's kingdom is about abundance, about multiplying, about giving with shocking generosity and still having leftovers. It's about taking the tiny offerings that our insecure hearts are willing to trust to Jesus and watching as He prays, thanks His Father, and then feeds everyone around us, including ourselves, with those small loaves and fish. His kingdom breaks and breaks and breaks our own expectations, always multiplying, always offering more, always blessing in astonishing, unexpected, jaw-dropping ways.

Satan wants you to be distracted into believing you have nothing to offer, to be disengaged, empty, and discouraged. Yet the Carpenter and Friend of fishermen who called a motley crew to follow Him and calls you and me each by name, wants all of you, every single breathing bit, to live its fullest, deepest, truest self in His kingdom. And to do that, He will deliberately break us open so that He can multiply all that we have available, all that we can bring to the kingdom table to feed the people around us.

He's not trying to take something away from us; His intention is to multiply what He's already given us. All our DNA that God has packed with potential and promise, He wants to see us share and spread. It's the ancient promise first spoken to Abram and then passed down through His children all the way to the Messiah and on to each of us, "I will bless you, I will make your name great, and you will be a blessing" (Gen. 12:2).

Take a moment. Look around your room. Think back on your day, and write down at least five things you have to be thankful for today—five ways God has dumped blessing into your life:

1.

2.

3.

4.

5.

Any blessing that shows up in our lives—from the breath that expands our lungs, the blood that runs through our veins, the children who wail in our living rooms, the work that waits at the end of long commutes, or the people who gather around our dining room tables and call us friends—every single one of these is a living picture of God's generosity to us. Given to bless us. And intended to bless others. **Blessings are not for hoarding; they're for forwarding.** Because that is how we reflect God's glory back to Him.

But being able to see beyond our own sense of entitlement, being willing to surrender what we want for what God wants is not an easy thing. Because if we focus on our own wants we're vulnerable to missing entirely what it is that God wants for us. Saul spent almost his entire kingship spectacularly failing to focus on anything beyond himself.

But where Saul failed, his son Jonathan lives on in history as probably the most selfless, others-focused friend ever recorded. And the hallmark of Jonathan's friendship and devotion to David was his relationship to and understanding of God. Even though he had rights to the kingship, he recognized the Lord's plan to anoint David as king so Jonathan trusted and lifted up David over himself. As the heir to Israel's throne, he had every right to have his own agenda, but instead, he pursued the Lord's and befriended David.

The *Halley's Bible Handbook* paints the picture that unfolds throughout the Book of 1 Samuel:

Jonathan was heir to the throne. His brilliant victory over the Philistines (chap. 14) and his nobility of character were good evidence that he would have made a worthy king. But he had found out that God had ordained David to be king, and his graceful self-effacement in giving up his succession to the throne and his unselfish devotion to David, whom he could have hated as a rival, form one of the noblest stories of friendship in history. Jonathan initiated a covenant with David, symbolized by the giving of robe, tunic, sword, bow, and belt. This act reflected Jonathan's recognition that David would take Jonathan's place as Saul's successor.[9]

Jonathan actively worked to advance what God was doing in and through David's life. He was able to ditch the giant chip of entitlement that his father carried everywhere to put his own agenda aside and lift up the one God had placed in front of him. I want so much to

be a friend who lifts up others because I see God's will in their lives. I don't want to miss that kind of holy assignment.

During David's darkest days, Jonathan—the man who could have been his chief competitor—was always there to encourage him. David had gone from being the most popular man in the kingdom to having a price put on his head—driven to live like a fugitive, hunted, ambushed, betrayed, forced away from his family and friends and living with the blood on his hands of the slaughter of those who tried to help him along the way (1 Sam. 22:6-19). He couldn't be sure of anyone; he doubted members of his own family. Saul was on his trail with a ruthless, senseless obsession to exterminate him. He was moving like a hunted rabbit from cave to cave seeking shelter and safety with no guarantee of either.

It's into this unique and desperate moment that his friend Jonathan risked his own life to bring David encouragement.

> Then Saul's son Jonathan came to David in Horesh and encouraged him in his faith in God, saying, "Don't be afraid, for my father Saul will never lay a hand on you. You yourself will be king over Israel, and I'll be your second-in-command. Even my father Saul knows it is true." Then the two of them made a covenant in the LORD's presence. Afterward, David remained in Horesh, while Jonathan went home.
> **1 SAMUEL 23:16-18**

Go back and circle the specific *actions* Jonathan took to encourage David.

Underline the specific *words for future encouragement* Jonathan spoke over David.

In one breath Jonathan affirmed God's call on David's life, assured David of his support, and made it clear that his allegiance wasn't a secret. Even his murderous father would know that Jonathan's loyalties lay with David.

At what must have been one of David's lowest moments, Jonathan was there to keep reminding him what God had called Him to do and how he was going to get there. He didn't take advantage of David's doubts and despairs to swoop in and snatch up what should have been his. No, where Saul was blinded by his jealousy, Jonathan was guided by His unwavering service to the Lord's anointed.

Now, if you're like me, then thinking like Jonathan doesn't just come naturally to us. Instead, we're susceptible to thinking, "But why can't I be the anointed one?" Yes? Have you felt like that before?

But here's the thing: you are. You actually already are an anointed one. How's that for a game changer?

> Just as Samuel anointed David, thousands of years later Jesus our new High Priest anoints us with His Holy Spirit. Write out 2 Corinthians 1:21.

Look, there's the same word *anointed*. This word was used in "commissioning service[s] that would symbolically set apart kings, prophets, priests, and special servants." In the same way, "the Holy Spirit sets apart believers and empowers them for the service of gospel proclamation and ministry."[10]

God's Holy Spirit on us is His mark of permanent calling and evidence of His salvation in our lives. We've been set apart to do the work He sets before us. We have been anointed to serve in God's kingdom, here and now, alongside others who have also been anointed and called. And that specifically includes the people in our lives who we've been given as friends. We've been called to lift up the exhausted arms of the people put in our lives on purpose. We've been anointed to serve our friends just as Jesus served His, just like Jonathan served David. So let's get to it, eh?

FRIENDSHIP CHALLENGE

Write the names of at least two of your friends. More if you'd like! Then under each name write down what you understand to be God's calling on their lives.

Now under that write down at least one way you can encourage and champion their work in a practical way this week. Repeat regularly.

Women aren't hungry for perfection; they're hungry for connection.

FRIENDSHIP TAKES SERVICE

Whoever wants to become great among you must be your servant, and whoever wants to be first among you must be your slave; just as the Son of Man did not come to be served, but to serve, and to give his life as a ransom for many.

MATTHEW 20:26-28

FRIENDSHIP TAKES SERVICE

VIEWER GUIDE: SESSION 4

Watch the Session 4 video and discuss with your group the following questions:

1. Share a personal experience, like Kristen and Deidra, about the difficulty of waiting on friendships to connect.

2. When have you seen the courage of "going first," or initiating friendship, pay off in your own life or for someone you know?

3. How has the perception of "cool kids" kept you from building relationships with others?

4. Read Matthew 20:20-28. What did Jesus teach His disciples about service?

5. How should we apply this lesson to our desire to be one of the "cool kids"?

6. Read Luke 6:31. What do we learn about service from this passage?

7. What are some practical ways you can serve your friends?

8. With your group, highlight any meaningful truths you took away from today's conversation at the table.

Video sessions available for purchase
at *LifeWay.com/WeSavedYouASeat*

STOP FIGHTING TO FIND A WAY IN

No matter how old we are, I think there's always going to be a teenage girl living inside of us desperate to be one of the cool kids. Define *cool* however you like, but often we can trace dissatisfied friendships to this search for the elusive "in" and dissatisfaction with where we find ourselves currently: a perceived "out."

The thing we don't realize in high school, and sometimes we still haven't learned during the minivan driving years, is that everyone is on the outside of something. But that is only half the story. We are all, each one of us, also on the inside of something—often without even realizing it.

So what we need to learn is that we can either fight to find a way in or we can love on the women right where we already are. We can obsess over who didn't talk to us or we can focus on the woman right in front of us. We can keep looking for a seat at a more popular table or we can pass the breadbasket and an introduction to the women sitting right beside us.

This week we want to remind ourselves that **asking someone to save you a seat at their table only to bypass them because you've spotted a seat at a more popular table can hurt you both.** So we're going to look at that teenager inside you deep in the eyes and cup hands gently around her tender, confused face and point her in the direction of all the *in* that's waiting for her. All the ways she's wanted. All the ways she belongs—if she can stop obsessing over her own wants and start focusing on loving the people around her. Letting people inside her invisible walls. And discovering she's been known and seen by the God who names her beloved all along.

As Jonathan served David, so Jesus served His friends. So we are called to follow in those humble footsteps and do the same, serving the people God has placed in our lives. Sometimes the best way to figure out what that looks like is to start with an example of what *not* to do.

Do you remember that show, "What Not To Wear"? I could watch that for hours. It was fascinating to see the transformation that went on when women's eyes were vulnerably, tearfully, frustratingly opened to what clothes were working against them. Stepping into that 360-degree mirror dressing room would not be anyone's idea of fun. But it was only when they truly saw themselves in their clothes from all angles for the first time that the participants started to accept the idea that maybe something needed to change.

I think we experience the same thing when it comes to what we're wearing on our souls. We might think we're motivated by friendship, encouragement, or generosity. But sometimes the truth is that we're motivated by entitlement or envy or fear. And we can't actually see all the angles of our motivations until someone holds a mirror up to us, gives us a glimpse of how badly those clothes fit, and offers clear guidelines for what style is intended for our souls instead.

On that note, let's first read a "What Not To Wear" story about soul clothing that is a terrible fit for Jesus' disciples and you and me:

> James and John, the sons of Zebedee, approached him and said,
> "Teacher, we want you to do whatever we ask you."
> "What do you want me to do for you?" he asked them.
> They answered him, "Allow us to sit at your right and at your left in
> your glory."
>
> Jesus said to them, "You don't know what you're asking." … When
> the ten disciples heard this, they began to be indignant with James
> and John.
> **MARK 10:35-38a,41**

In other words, the other ten were flat out furious. How dare two brothers try to shoulder everyone else out of the way for the prime real estate at Jesus' side? What soft spot did this behavior hit?

Can you put into your own words what you think James and John were really asking for in this passage, and why?

Have you ever done something similar? When?

We all do it, don't we? Jockeying for position, for the best seat at the best table. It's the kind of prestige grab we are often too subtle, or too polite, or too passive aggressive to say out loud. But Jesus hears it nonetheless.

For me, it can sound like, "Please, Jesus, choose me for that writing assignment, send me to that speaking opportunity, give me that chance to step into the spotlight, light me up with invitations like You've done for her. Set me up on a throne or a headline." It boils down to the same thing, doesn't it?

But Jesus patiently teaches me over and over again how gross that greedy spirit is. And He models His own version of what to wear on our souls and in our friendships.

> Jesus called them over and said to them, "You know that those who are regarded as rulers of the Gentiles lord it over them and those in high positions act as tyrants over them. But it is not so among you. On the contrary, whoever wants to become great among you will be your servant, and whoever wants to be first among you will be a slave to all. For even the Son of Man did not come to be served, but to serve, and to give his life as a ransom for many."
> MARK 10:42-45

And then this one from John. This passage that explodes my head and my heart any time I read it because the logic is so *utterly* other worldly. So impossible for us to grasp. Such brilliant teaching through doing that it sinks the lesson deep into our self-centered hearts. In the exact opposite soul clothing that His disciples modeled, this is what Jesus reflects.

> ³ Jesus knew that the Father had given everything into his hands, that he had come from God, and that he was going back to God. ⁴ So he got up from supper, laid aside his outer clothing, took a towel, and tied it around himself. ⁵ Next, he poured water into a basin and began to wash his disciples' feet and to dry them with the towel tied around him.
> JOHN 13:3-5

What are the four things Jesus did in verse 4?

1.

2.

3.

4.

What are the three things He does next in verse 5?

1.

2.

3.

I can't even read it without tears prickling in my eyes, because it's so humiliating. To be willing to kneel before the sweaty feet of men who spent all day walking dirt roads in sandals, often doubting you and trying to get something from you. And to do it knowing full well what your identity is, how you are descended from kings—both mortal and immortal! Why this moves me so much is that Jesus humbled Himself because He so fully understood where His identity truly lay. Knowing that everything He had and everything He was—His entire identity—was held safely in the hands of the Father meant that instead of grasping for recognition, He was able to open His hands and serve the people in front of Him. All power and prestige had been placed in His hands by the Father, but Jesus didn't clench His fists around them. Instead He opened His hands and released all of His claims to fame so that He could pick up a washcloth and bar of soap to serve the dirty feet and broken people in front of Him.

AFTER THIS ASTONISHING ACT OF SERVICE, READ WHAT JESUS DOES NEXT IN JOHN 13.

When Jesus had washed their feet and put on his outer clothing, he reclined again and said to them, "Do you know what I have done for you? You call me Teacher and Lord—and you are speaking rightly, since that is what I am. So if I, your Lord and Teacher, have washed your feet, you also ought to wash one another's feet. For I have given you an example, that you also should do just as I have done for you. Truly I tell you, a servant is not greater than his master, and a messenger is not greater than the one who sent him."
JOHN 13:12-16

That is how we serve our friends and our own souls. And this is what to wear.

Therefore, as God's chosen ones, holy and dearly loved, put on compassion, kindness, humility, gentleness, and patience, bearing with one another and forgiving one another if anyone has a grievance against another. Just as the Lord has forgiven you, so you are also to forgive. Above all, put on love, which is the perfect bond of unity. And let the peace of Christ, to which you were also called in one body, rule your hearts. And be thankful.
COLOSSIANS 3:12-15

What does this example teach us to clothe ourselves with? Write down the various items of soul clothing listed in these verses.

FRIENDSHIP CHALLENGE

Consider your friendships this week. Pay attention to the kind of soul clothing you're wearing around them. And bear with me as I pretend we have two closets in front of us. On the left side of the page, list the kind of soul clothes you want to be done with and kick out of your closet—the "What NOT To Wears" in a friendship. Then, on the right side of the page list the kind of soul clothes you'd like to stock your closet. Because, you can, you know. We only have to ask and Jesus will meet our needs with His own wildly generous spirit of service.

WHAT NOT TO WEAR IN FRIENDSHIP	WHAT TO WEAR IN FRIENDSHIP

FEED THE PEOPLE AT YOUR TABLE

I don't know about you but when I think about the words *service, calling, following Jesus,* or *discipleship* I don't always think about my refrigerator. Or my dining room table. Definitely not about my toilet or bathroom. I tend to think far off fuzzy thoughts about important titles and business cards, auditoriums, book contracts, or radio interviews. And then there's an afternoon when Play-Doh® is strewn all over the floor in hard little dribs and drabs, the counters are covered in plates, and there have been a steady stream of people through our house by the end of the week, and it shows. Then, I remember, that this is what service mostly looks like.

We are everyday ministers of the gospel. It shows up in our homes like neighbor kids, friends who need a ride to the airport, hosting a home group, making a meal for a friend, or even better, welcoming a stranger at church. We can become blind to our own ministry that takes place every single day outside the spotlight but is caught in the bright glare of heaven's gaze.

Because that's where we will actually make our names. A name for being the place where neighbor kids feel welcome showing up unannounced. A name for opening the door even when it's inconvenient. A name for making time, giving time, being available. Because our open front doors and sometimes nearly-bare refrigerators and sticky dining room tables will be the places we literally practice what we preach before we dare go take that message anywhere else.

I'm not always that good at making this obvious connection. I get irritated and tired and I like my own personal space. Admittedly, there are days I want to be wanted by important people with important titles more than I want to open my fridge to visitors who know me by name and have seen me in my Saturday afternoon sweatpants. But while I may have those thoughts, I don't want them to be the boss of me.

I want my dining room table to be the boss of me, especially when I'm tempted to set my sights on something "better" than my right now, right here friends and neighbors. That table with the big, wide, country planks that have crumbs filling up the cracks. That table with the squeaky chairs we constantly have to repair. That table that can seat stray college students and Tuesday night friends. That table that is doing its best work when it's messy and has sticky streaks and an extra bench added down one side. That table and my front door are teaching me that the one seat I need to focus on is the one next to me, not the one across the room or the aisle or even the other end of the table. It's the seat right next to me right now that is supposed to be my teacher. Whether my best friend, a new friend, a relative, a stranger, or one of my own children is sitting in it.

Dear God, please help us not to miss the beauty of the seat right next to us. Help us to stop worrying about being impressive and instead to feed the hungry who show up at our tables. To feed them our best, our friendship, our time. To feed them our patience, our interest, our availability. Perhaps our friendships are only as big and deep as our hospitality. And I'm not talking about our decor or our skills in the kitchen. I'm talking about our willingness to invite people in despite our decor, not because of it.

This is living. Not just the making room for it with clean floors and plates, toothbrushes put away, and sinks wiped down. (*Why on earth can't they ever remember to rinse the sink?* I mutter every night.) No, this is what those spaces are made for. They hold room for the people. And it's the people who make us extraordinary.

These people are always a gift and a living, breathing reminder of the imprint of God left uniquely and divinely on each of them. I have a serving tray in my house that has Hebrews 13:2 painted onto it. Write, color, or illustrate that verse.

Now write down the names of the people who you've come into contact with this week—the neighbor kids, the PTA moms, the book club friends, the cubicle next door to yours, and the people who live under your roof. Let's write down their names so that we're consciously paying attention to them now.

I think too often I've kept one eye on the door, waiting to be amazed by strangers who might come my way. When really it's those I know best—the most familiar and sometimes the most irritating—I most take for granted, who are the most holy representatives of God with us, Immanuel.

When God moved into the neighborhood through His Son, Jesus, He literally became the kid next door, the friend from Temple, the nephew, the grandson, the brother, the teacher, the best friend, the preacher. He was so ordinary in His regular, everyday roles that it stretched the imagination too much for those who knew Him best to see anything worth paying attention to in His message or His example.

> He went to his hometown and began to teach them in their synagogue, so that they were astonished and said, "Where did this man get this wisdom and these miraculous powers? Isn't this the carpenter's son? Isn't his mother called Mary, and his brothers James, Joseph, Simon, and Judas? And his sisters, aren't they all with us? So where does he get all these things?" And they were offended by him. Jesus said to them, "A prophet is not without honor except in his hometown and in his household." And he did not do many miracles there because of their unbelief.
> **MATTHEW 13:54-58**

Don't believe that your people and your place are ordinary for a minute. Your life is so full of glory it will weigh you down if you just stop to feel it every once in awhile, if you stop to let it sink down deep into your here and now.

I don't want to make the mistake of ignoring the people right in front of me, the people who sometimes show up like neighbor kids with their soccer balls at inconvenient times, and my job is simply to open the front door. I can do this. I'm the only one who can do this because this is my house and my yard and I've been given this little plot in God's kingdom. It's my job to be a good and generous host here. Forget about conferences and stages. If I can't pull out a welcoming chair at my very own dining room table, what business do I have opening a Bible or a book or a message anywhere else?

All through Scripture the central theme from Adam to Noah to Abraham to Ruth to David to Jesus to the disciples to the nations to us is the theme of being redeemed by God for the singular purpose of becoming a witness of that same grace, mercy, and blessing to others. Over and over the promise is given that we are blessed so that we can become a blessing to everyone around us (Gen. 22:17-18). And we can start by simply opening our front doors.

Introduce yourself to the woman sitting next to you. Pay attention to your friends' lives, asking questions, showing interest, taking time to study the people you've started taking for granted because you're so familiar with them. You may be surprised by how deciding to take an extra, intentional step toward them today changes things for both of you. Not because there's a crisis or occasion. Just because you want to connect on purpose.

FRIENDSHIP CHALLENGE

Who are the people in your life you think you may have been taking for granted lately?

How can you or have you taken them for granted?

What practical, fun, "just because" kind of ways can you reinvest in that relationship again?

When was the last time you felt like the "new girl"?

When was the last time you had a chance to include a "new girl" in your circle? What did you do?

If you're currently in a "new girl" season of life, what is one way you can show up and connect with your local community to begin plugging in?

If you have a "new girl" in your circle, what practical ways can you deliberately include her this week?

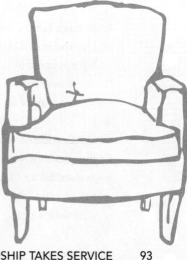

LOVE LIKE YOU WANT TO BE LOVED

OK, here it is. This is the secret to finding and keeping lasting friendships: Become women who want to see the women around them flourish.

> Here is a simple rule of thumb for behavior: Ask yourself what you want people to do for you; then grab the initiative and do it for *them!*
> LUKE 6:31, MSG

They have a word for that in Hebrew—it's *shalom*. But not *shalom* like you might think. Not the overused, under-appreciated translation that we're so used to throwing around as the word *peace*. As in the opposite of conflict. Instead, this word is used more than 200 times throughout Scripture in a radically more interactive way.

The kind of *shalom* we're challenged to give to the people around us requires us to take an active interest in their physical and spiritual well-being. When you look up the various translations to understand how the word is used, *shalom* means caring about someone else's safety and soundness in body, welfare, prosperity, peace and contentment, friendship and good health—to name just a few—as well as caring deeply about seeing conflict come to an end.

Shalom is passionately invested in seeking the well-being of others—other people, places, cultures, and neighbors. It's about leaning into the Great Commission to become a blessing to the people around us.

Shalom is a radical word that challenges us to wake up from our obsession with ourselves and instead start the deliberate choice of focusing on the people around us, desperately caring less about ourselves and more about them.

Let's go on a bit of a treasure hunt through Scripture to see how and where the word *shalom* turns up. We'll just sample a few key passages since *shalom* is used so many times throughout the Bible and is translated into a variety of English transliterations. The English words *well* and *peace* are just a few examples of how the Hebrew word *shalom* has been transliterated.

Highlight the word *well* every time it appears in the following verses. Then, based on the context of the larger story, write in your own words what you think the speaker means when they're using the word *well* in the verses below.

"Do you know Laban grandson of Nahor?" Jacob asked them.
They answered, "We know him."
"Is he well?" Jacob asked.
GENESIS 29:5-6a

What the speaker means:

And Israel said to Joseph, "Are not your brothers pasturing the flock at Shechem? Come, I will send you to them." And he said to him, "Here I am." So he said to him, "Go now, see if it is well with your brothers and with the flock, and bring me word."
GENESIS 37:13-14, ESV

What the speaker means:

Moses went out to meet his father-in-law and bowed down and kissed him. And they asked each other of their welfare and went into the tent.
EXODUS 18:7, ESV

What the speaker means:

And Jesse said to David his son, "Take for your brothers an ephah of this parched grain, and these ten loaves, and carry them quickly to the camp to your brothers. Also take these ten cheeses to the commander of their thousand. See if your brothers are well, and bring some token from them."
1 SAMUEL 17:17-18, ESV

What the speaker means:

When the man of God saw her coming, he said to Gehazi his servant, "Look, there is the Shunammite. Run at once to meet her and say to her, 'Is all well with you? Is all well with your husband? Is all well with the child?'" And she answered, "All is well."
2 KINGS 4:25b-26, ESV

What the speaker means:

When Jesse sent his teenage son, David, out from his daily grind among their bleating, flock of sheep to go and check on his brothers who were fighting at the front lines of King Saul's army, he was sending David to check up on their *shalom*—to see how they were doing physically—did they have enough to eat? He also wanted to see how they were doing spiritually—were they discouraged? How was their mood, their sense of hope, their faith in the outcome of the battle?

The same word appears in the New Testament and is also translated *peace*. Underline that word *peace* where it appears in these verses. In your own words, record what you think the author was trying to communicate by using the word here:

It's the same word that appears as the angels announce Jesus' birth.

> Glory to God in the highest heaven,
> and peace on earth to people he favors!
> LUKE 2:14

What the speaker means:

It's the same word Jesus used in His intimate sermon to His disciples when He told them,

> Blessed are the peacemakers,
> for they will be called sons of God.
> MATTHEW 5:9

What the speaker means:

The "*shalom* makers." Those who are invested, interested, and diligently working for the well-being of the people around them, "for they will be called sons of God" (Matt. 5:9). Because choosing this hard and deliberate course of caring about the lives of the people around you, of being a peacemaker, is to walk in the footsteps of the God man, Jesus. The *shalom* maker who actively, deliberately stepped into every day of His life on earth, choosing our well-being over His own even beyond the point when it cost Him His own life.

That's the gospel. We are at peace so we can be peace. We've been invested in so that we can invest.

So, what can you do to find safe, loving, engaged friends who you can trust never to unfriend you? Become radically invested in the people around you. Take the initiative and become that kind of friend first.

Stop keeping score—who called who last, who owes who an email or a play date or a lunch date—and start initiating. Friendship isn't something we passively receive. Friendship is something we actively do. It's a gift we offer for free, not a demand we make with a stamping foot. We love others well because of how well we have been loved ourselves.

READ JOHN 13:34 AND RECORD IT IN YOUR OWN WORDS.

FRIENDSHIP CHALLENGE

Write down the names of two women you care about. It doesn't even matter if they are your close friends or not.

Now write down two specific ways in which you can invest in their *shalom*, their well-being. Get down to the nitty gritty. What do they need in their lives to flourish, to draw closer to God, and to become the people God created them to be? How can you help facilitate that this week?

Here are some ideas to kick off your own brainstorming about how you can serve and support your friends:

- ☐ Write her a text message, email, or note listing specific ways you see her walking in her calling.
- ☐ Ask her one practical way you can encourage her this week—does she need help with babysitting, a friend to pray with, a chance to talk through an idea with someone?
- ☐ Is there a gift you could give her that shows how much you believe in who she is in the Lord? A journal or a gift card to her favorite coffee shop, art supply store, or for gas on her commute into work?
- ☐ In what ways can you publicly share with other friends the work she has done or is doing that you're so proud of?

Without
FORGIVENESS,
Friendship
BECOMES
— EXTINCT. —

FRIENDSHIP TAKES FORGIVENESS

If anyone says, "I love God," and yet hates his brother or sister, he is a liar. For the person who does not love his brother or sister whom he has seen cannot love God whom he has not seen.

1 JOHN 4:20

Friendship takes Forgiveness

VIEWER GUIDE: SESSION 5

Watch the Session 5 video and discuss with your group the following questions:

1. How have you seen past relationships affect your current relationships?

2. Read 1 John 4:20. What does this passage reveal about the necessity of forgiveness?

3. Lisa-Jo noted the emotional, psychological, and spiritual benefits of forgiveness. How have you seen the positive effects of forgiveness?

4. Kristen talked about choosing forgiveness and acting on it, even when we don't feel the emotions of forgiveness. Discuss with your group some ways you can choose forgiveness and act upon it, even when the feelings aren't behind the action just yet.

5. How do you see grief, as Deidra addressed, as part of the forgiveness process?

6. How have you seen unforgiveness reappear in your life later on?

7. What kind of effect has unforgiveness had on you or others?

8. How do you see forgiveness as an act of courage?

9. With your group, highlight any meaningful truths you took away from today's conversation at the table.

Video sessions available for purchase
at *LifeWay.com/WeSavedYouASeat*

DON'T LET YOUR PAST HURTS POISON YOUR CURRENT FRIENDSHIPS.

Even if you show up for friendship, even if you open your front door and invite people into your real, messy life and make time and welcome interruptions because you meant it when you said you really want friends, friendship can still end up hurting you. More specifically, at some point Christian women will hurt you—as will non-Christian women. Hopefully not on purpose. Hopefully through simple ignorance or their own insecurity. But sometimes, sadly, it will have been on purpose. But either way, what then? How do we remain open to friendship when friendship has taken advantage of our vulnerability and hurt us?

Do we close our front doors and our hearts, or do we keep trusting God and His invitation to love other people and let them in? Because if we haven't been able to trust other people, if they've let us down and if they've hurt us—by accident, and sometimes worse, on purpose—how can we keep putting ourselves out there?

How have you been hurt by a friend?

How do you think it's affected your subsequent friendships?

I don't know about you, but I have definitely had those friendships that have left my heart tender and my soul suspicious. When you've been badly wounded by a woman you thought was your friend I think you're susceptible to a kind of friendship PTSD (post-traumatic stress disorder).

In his book, *Social Intelligence: The New Science of Human Relationships,* Daniel Goleman explains why. Every social interaction reshapes our brains through what is called neuroplasticity. In other words, just like we learn not to touch that lighted candle after we get burned the first time or how we might enjoy repeating the habit of late night TV bingeing and ice cream, repeated social experiences teach us which relationships are hot to the touch and which ones are delicious.[1]

First as little girls and then as teens and adults, the patterns we live over and over again in our friendships aren't by accident. They're the actual rewiring of our brains to connect or not connect based on past experiences. So if we've had a defining relationship that ended up exploding our hearts, we're more likely to experience some degree of post-traumatic stress when we find ourselves in a similar relationship situation in the future.

The thing is our friendship PTSD can be the reason we're missing out on connecting with new friends or going deeper with our current friends. It can be the reason we haul a huge suitcase of friendship baggage along with us every time we walk into the conversation.

I believe if it were up to him, Satan would like nothing more than to see all us women infected by our past hurts and the grudges we lug around with us. If it were up to Satan, he would strap all our failed friendships and all those times our trust was disappointed onto our backs and have us carry them into every conversation, tender connection, and new interaction, into every Bible study and book club, and into every girls' night out.

We can cripple a friendship before it even begins by piling the baggage of all our previous relationships onto it.

That friendship that ended badly, that misunderstanding, that time you were left out that you can't seem to get over—are you still dragging those around with you? Are they still causing you friendship PTSD?

Let's pause there for a minute. Let's ask the Holy Spirit to show us what friendship baggage we're still holding onto.

Will you pray with me?

Father,

I trust You with my heart. I trust You with my past. And I ask You to gently show me if there are pieces of my own anger or disappointment or hurt that I'm still holding onto from past friendship failures. Will You help me see it too? So that I can let it go. So that I can stop dragging all that pain into each of my new relationships. Will You please set me free? Will You defuse the memories I'm walking around with and give me a new friendship story?

Amen.

NOW LET'S READ JOHN 10:10 TOGETHER.

A thief comes only to steal and kill and destroy. I have come so that they may have life and have it in abundance.
JOHN 10:10

What has Jesus promised to come and bring us?

What kind of life did He come to give us?

He's the only one who can cut that dead weight of broken relationships and old patterns off our backs and invite us into community with Him, setting us free to embrace friendship. He is not a stingy God. He is generous in all areas. Why wouldn't He be generous in the area of friendship too?

You prepare a table before me
in the presence of my enemies;
you anoint my head with oil;
my cup overflows.
PSALM 23:5

God's generosity:

If you then, who are evil, know how to give good gifts to your children,
how much more will your Father in heaven give good things to those
who ask him.
MATTHEW 7:11

God's generosity:

Give, and it will be given to you; a good measure—pressed down,
shaken together, and running over—will be poured into your lap.
For with the measure you use, it will be measured back to you.
LUKE 6:38

God's generosity:

As much as He understands life and generosity, if anyone understands friendship betrayal, it is also Jesus. Betrayed by one of His own disciples and disowned by His closest friends, Jesus' wounds are real. They are raw. But Jesus won't let us stop there. He won't let us live in the place where we're the victim constantly pointing fingers. No, He wants us to follow in His wounded footsteps, to the place where we are willing to forgive, because it's the only way through to life.

> For you were called to this, because Christ also suffered for you, leaving you an example, that you should follow in his steps.
> 1 PETER 2:21

> Then Jesus said to his disciples, "Whoever wants to be my disciple must deny themselves and take up their cross and follow me."
> MATTHEW 16:24, NIV

That's what this first day is about: simply preparing our hearts to be willing to walk in Jesus' footsteps, because forgiveness is very hard. It may be one of the hardest spiritual disciplines we have to put into practice. And it's not easy to just jump right into it. So today is simply about pausing and recognizing your hurts and preparing your heart for what comes next—either bearing a grudge or accepting Jesus' offer of life and freedom through forgiveness. Those are the only two choices.

FRIENDSHIP CHALLENGE

Grab a stack of scrap paper, sticky notes, or index cards. Now, remember those past hurts from friendship that the Holy Spirit brought to your mind when we prayed earlier and write them down. One per piece of paper. Write down what happened, what was done to you. Be specific about your disappointments. Write down all the ways that you felt let down or overlooked or taken for granted by a friend (past or current). Just get it all out—bleed your hurts onto the pages.

Now, I want you to read those bits of paper out loud. We bear witness to how you were hurt. We don't discount it. We don't try to brush it off or excuse it. We see it, friend. We see it, and we acknowledge that it hurt. It's OK to cry. It's OK to ache. Take all the time you need.

And once you've caught your breath, tuck those scraps of paper into an envelope and put them into your Bible for safekeeping. We'll come back to them on Day 3, OK? This is how we prepare our hearts for what comes next. This is how we take a first step to being ready to give and receive forgiveness.

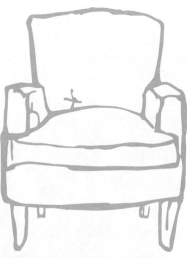

BE BRAVE ENOUGH TO ASK FOR FORGIVENESS

There are no perfect people. Inevitably someone will hurt us, and we will hurt someone. What matters is what comes next. Will we forgive them, or will we withdraw? Will we work it out, or will we write it off? We are all broken and wounded, but only by choosing to say sorry or receive someone else's apology can we begin to grow deep roots into a friendship.

Forgiveness is always ground zero when it comes to any relationship, especially friendship. Let's take a moment to think about that.

What are your friendship habits when the going gets tough? When you've been hurt by a friend do you (check all that apply):

☐ Cut and run
☐ Dial up the passive aggressive behavior until she realizes something is wrong
☐ Pretend like nothing happened
☐ Confront her—via email, text, or in person
☐ Avoid her until the friendship fades away
☐ Make time to talk it out with her

Now what about if you're the one who has hurt a friend. Whether it was unintentional or because of your own careless behavior. Whether you believe what you did warrants someone being hurt or not, if she approaches you, what is your response in that situation? Do you (check all that apply):

☐ Become defensive

☐ Make excuses and point out all the ways you are also the victim

☐ Ignore the issue

☐ Dodge the conversation altogether so she never has a chance to connect with you

☐ Take the time to listen and understand and ask for forgiveness

☐ Feel so bad that the awkwardness interferes with the future of the friendship

☐ Decide that the friendship isn't worth "the drama"

Looking at that checklist, it might seem really obvious what the right choices are. But as we all know, real life, real time conversations about hurt can be really awkward. They are hard to navigate and hard to come back from, but choosing whether or not to ask for forgiveness or grant forgiveness will make or break a relationship. Literally.

And because we're good at recognizing our own hurts but can sometimes have a blind spot when it comes to how we've hurt other people, let's start there.

Before we move on to what it looks like for us to extend forgiveness, let's spend some time on the more awkward and self-conscious subject of what it looks like for us to ask for forgiveness—what it looks like when we're the ones in the wrong. (If you can't think of a time you've ever been in the wrong in a friendship, then I think this chapter is especially for you.)

As I've studied forgiveness over the past year I've been so struck by the different responses of two of Jesus' disciples to their own friendship failures. Peter and Judas both betrayed Jesus. Both hurt the man they claimed as a friend. Both despaired, both wept, both wished they could undo what they had done. But one was swallowed up in despair and took his own life while the other came to Jesus for forgiveness and to have his life restored.

Let's spend some time with these two men.

Let's retrace those terrible three days and nights to see how they each responded when confronted with how they'd betrayed their best friend.

READ EACH OF THE VERSES IN THEIR TIME LINES AND CONNECT THE DOTS OF WHAT UNFOLDED DURING ONE OF THE MOST NOTORIOUS STORIES OF BETRAYAL OF ALL TIME. FILL IN THE BLANKS WITH THE BEHAVIOR BY JUDAS AND PETER RESPECTIVELY:

JESUS PREDICTS THE BETRAYAL OF BOTH JUDAS AND PETER

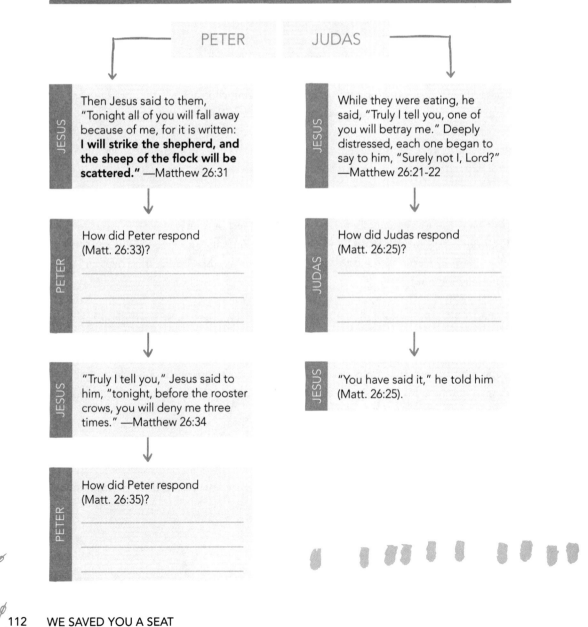

PETER   JUDAS

JESUS
Then Jesus said to them, "Tonight all of you will fall away because of me, for it is written: **I will strike the shepherd, and the sheep of the flock will be scattered."** —Matthew 26:31

JESUS
While they were eating, he said, "Truly I tell you, one of you will betray me." Deeply distressed, each one began to say to him, "Surely not I, Lord?" —Matthew 26:21-22

PETER
How did Peter respond (Matt. 26:33)?
_____
_____
_____

JUDAS
How did Judas respond (Matt. 26:25)?
_____
_____
_____

JESUS
"Truly I tell you," Jesus said to him, "tonight, before the rooster crows, you will deny me three times." —Matthew 26:34

JESUS
"You have said it," he told him (Matt. 26:25).

PETER
How did Peter respond (Matt. 26:35)?
_____
_____
_____

JUDAS AND PETER BETRAY JESUS

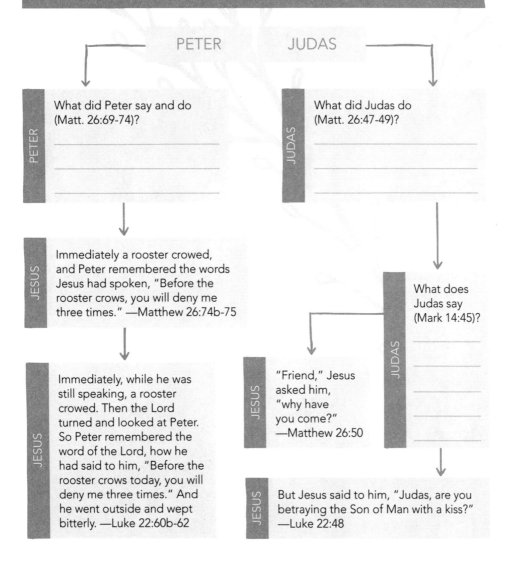

PETER

JUDAS

PETER

What did Peter say and do (Matt. 26:69-74)?

_____

_____

_____

JUDAS

What did Judas do (Matt. 26:47-49)?

_____

_____

_____

JESUS

Immediately a rooster crowed, and Peter remembered the words Jesus had spoken, "Before the rooster crows, you will deny me three times." —Matthew 26:74b-75

JUDAS

What does Judas say (Mark 14:45)?

_____

_____

_____

JESUS

Immediately, while he was still speaking, a rooster crowed. Then the Lord turned and looked at Peter. So Peter remembered the word of the Lord, how he had said to him, "Before the rooster crows today, you will deny me three times." And he went outside and wept bitterly. —Luke 22:60b-62

JESUS

"Friend," Jesus asked him, "why have you come?" —Matthew 26:50

JESUS

But Jesus said to him, "Judas, are you betraying the Son of Man with a kiss?" —Luke 22:48

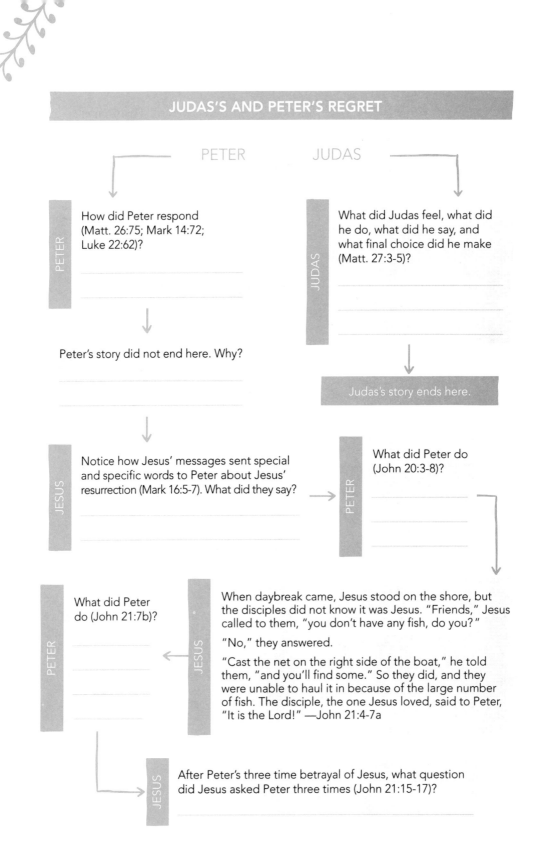

JUDAS'S AND PETER'S REGRET

PETER   JUDAS

PETER

How did Peter respond (Matt. 26:75; Mark 14:72; Luke 22:62)?

_____

_____

JUDAS

What did Judas feel, what did he do, what did he say, and what final choice did he make (Matt. 27:3-5)?

_____

_____

_____

Peter's story did not end here. Why?

_____

_____

Judas's story ends here.

JESUS

Notice how Jesus' messages sent special and specific words to Peter about Jesus' resurrection (Mark 16:5-7). What did they say?

_____

_____

_____

PETER

What did Peter do (John 20:3-8)?

_____

_____

PETER

What did Peter do (John 21:7b)?

_____

_____

JESUS

When daybreak came, Jesus stood on the shore, but the disciples did not know it was Jesus. "Friends," Jesus called to them, "you don't have any fish, do you?"

"No," they answered.

"Cast the net on the right side of the boat," he told them, "and you'll find some." So they did, and they were unable to haul it in because of the large number of fish. The disciple, the one Jesus loved, said to Peter, "It is the Lord!" —John 21:4-7a

JESUS

After Peter's three time betrayal of Jesus, what question did Jesus asked Peter three times (John 21:15-17)?

_____

What does all this mean? Is there really some similarity between these two men and their stories? I've become so fascinated by them this year. I've leaned in as close as I could to peer back through the pages of history to try to understand how their betrayals had such radically different endings. And the more I read, the more I study, the more convinced I am that each of their unique plot twists hinge on whether or not they believed Jesus could and would forgive them. We've retraced their footsteps in the chart above, now let's decode what their actions meant.

Without any trace of irony, Jesus called Judas His friend right on the very doorstep of his betrayal. Their was no echo of judgment in Jesus' words. The word *friend* here is "an openhearted but not intimate greeting."[2] This is simply the honesty of a God who is publicly acknowledging the truth of His own predictions. Eye to eye, cheek to cheek, Judas had to face the truth about himself in Jesus' eyes and words. Some word studies go further though and suggest the Greek word Jesus used here (*hetairos*) implied the kind of friend who is "viewed (associated) as a friend, but is actually an imposter acting for self-gain."[3]

And then there's Peter who, as the rooster crowed, looked into the eyes of his friend, the man He had sworn to defend with His very life, and saw the reflection of His own failure and Jesus' prediction realized. But the commentaries tell us there wasn't any condemnation in Jesus' gaze. Instead, much like His interaction with Judas, it seems that Jesus felt compassion for Peter:

In telling how the Lord looked at Peter (v. 61), Luke uses the [same] word John used (see John 1:42) to describe the way Jesus looked at Peter when they first met. It "usually signifies a look of interest, love or concern."[4]

Both Judas and Peter were devastated. They were crushed. They wept bitterly. They mourned, grieved, and neither tried to defend himself. But here's the crux of the difference between their shockingly different outcomes—Judas was crushed by the weight of his own guilt, and it killed him. But Peter, oh Peter. He went running and splashing, guilt and all, to Jesus.

Judas went to the chief priests and elders for absolution and when he couldn't get it, he took it upon himself to judge himself. And the weight was too terrible to bear.

Maybe Judas's terrible act of self-judgment and condemnation has some echoes of familiarity—for those of us who find we can hardly move for the weight of our own crushing guilt.

How are you enacting judgment on yourself? Do you binge eat? Do you purge? Do you cut? Is there a constant stream of criticism in your head raging against yourself? Friends, it's time to bring all your self-hatred to the Friend who will forgive you.

Stop trying to carry it all by yourself.

Stop trying to punish yourself.

Stop hating yourself.

It's time to make like Peter and run to Jesus. Run as fast as your tired and disappointed legs can carry you to the God of the empty tomb, to the God who carries life in His very bones.

Will we be brave enough to bring our friendship failures, sins, and selfish behavior to the Savior who can resurrect them? Or will we be crushed by our own disappointments and run away from the friendships that try to make us face them?

FRIENDSHIP CHALLENGE

Is there something you need to ask forgiveness for? Is there a relational sin that's haunting you? A sin that's crushing you with its weight, that's trying to choke the very life out of you? A careless sin? A sin that hurt a friend and broke a friendship? Bring that sin to Jesus. Don't avoid Him. He already knows. He's already seen.

He's leaned His cheek up close to your own cheek right in the very act of your sinning. Turn and meet His gaze and tell Him you're sorry. It's OK. He loves you. He can radically redeem your life the way He did Peter's. God wants you in His kingdom and He gave His own Son's life to get you there.

Write a prayer to Jesus and ask for forgiveness. Then go and ask forgiveness if you've hurt any of His daughters. Asking forgiveness is an act of courage. Come to the God of the empty tomb and let Him wash you clean and send you whole and healthy back into friendship.

IF WE LOVE GOD, WE CAN'T HATE OUR FRIENDS.

There is a reason that the Lord's Prayer first talks about asking for forgiveness for ourselves and then, once we're free of our own debts, it moves to forgiving the debts owed against us. In the world of friendships that we want to invest in deeply, asking forgiveness is step one. Then once we've received what we know we didn't deserve, extending the same grace and forgiving the people around us is step two. Because to hate the people around you is to hate the image of God in them. Jesus, the God-man who had more reason to hate, resent, and nurture bitterness than any of us, constantly, deliberately, ruthlessly loved those who hurt Him and consistently chose love over the easier choice of hate. Are we brave enough to follow in Jesus' footsteps? Because His challenge to love our neighbor as ourselves is intimidating. Because it has resounding ramifications.

Write out 1 John 4:20.

Forgiveness is an act of generosity. It's passing everything that we've freely been given onto someone else. Without forgiveness, friendship becomes extinct and relationship non-existent. In his book about the new science of human relationships, Daniel Goleman calls forgiveness an "antidote" to the "lasting biological consequence[s]" of cycles of rage, hurt, and revenge. Forgiving someone who has hurt us actually reverses those biological reactions: lowering blood pressure, heart rate, and levels of stress hormones as well as lessening pain and depression.[5]

In my own experience, however, there's something of a sliding scale for how hard it will be to forgive someone. On the one end of the scale are the people who hurt us unwittingly. They didn't plan to hurt us. They hurt us by accident, by being careless with our feelings or completely ignorant of what the impact of their actions were. These are the people we trust and who deep down in our gut we know are rooting for our best. And knowing that they never meant to hurt us goes a long way in helping us forgive them.

Describe a situation in which you knew a person haphazardly hurt you. How did you know it was an accident?

Were you able to forgive them easily? Why?

However, on the other end of that sliding scale is a dark and wretched place—because there lie the hurts caused by people on purpose. Or by people who were so cavalier with our hearts that even if we tried to show them our open wounds, they'd shrug their shoulders and go back to their coffee.

Beth Moore describes in wrenching words the exact feelings I've had in those situations:

How often have I made a fool of myself just trying to get someone who hurt me to hear me?[6]

The deep injustice of being wounded by someone who doesn't care or isn't interested in understanding our pain can feel like acid burning away your skin. You feel stripped, emotionally bare, skin raw and flaming with the unfairness of it all.

On the day I was baptized I had someone walk up to me and hand me a card. And what I thought was going to be a note full of love and affirmation and finally reconciliation from someone who had haunted my life with misery for months turned out to be a blistering outburst of condemnation and ugliness. Handed to me in church. On the day I was publicly dedicating my life to the Lord. Twenty years later I can still feel the impact of that slap.

On the day Joseph was sent out to check on his brothers and bring them word from their father, their hatred boiled over while he was still at a distance. Their anger then grew hands and fingers that stripped off his "robe of many colors" the moment he arrived and threw him into a deep pit in the earth (Gen. 37:23). After plotting the death of their little brother they casually, "sat down to eat a meal" (v. 25). The Amplified Bible describes the haunting scene well:

> We saw the distress *and* anguish of his soul when he pleaded with us [to let him go], yet we would not listen [to his cry].
> GENESIS 42:21, AMP

The terrible injustice of people in your life who move from hurting you to dishing up supper without ever taking a breath in between to say they're sorry can make you sick.

Forgiveness will not necessarily be easy, but it is necessary. And ultimately it will be more satisfying than revenge. Because,

Forgiveness is not passivity, dear one. It is power. It is the ability to withstand the pressing, quaking gates of hell. Take this power and wield it. It's your right as a child of God. In the power of Jesus, first you will it and soon you'll feel it.[7]

But how? How do we grope our way to forgiveness? Not because we want to or even because we're capable, but we forgive because there are giant footprints we can sink our desperate feet into. We can walk in the shoes of Christ because He did it first. Jesus forgave. While being tortured He looked out into the faces of His torturers and said the immortal words,

> Father, forgive them, because they do not know what they are doing.
> LUKE 23:34

This is only possible because forgiveness is not about a feeling but about a willing. Forgiveness sent Christ to the cross, where He willingly was beaten, spat upon, and nailed by us and for us. The God-man could've said, "Forget this," but instead He bowed His head and generously and unfairly took upon Himself your sin and my sin. And to the ones who had directly hurt Him, He immediately offered them forgiveness.

Forgiveness. As Beth Moore wrote, "No stronger force exists."[8]

Christ chose to forgive them—and us—because He knew that they didn't have a clue. Beth Moore writes,

Whoever threw you into the pit doesn't have any idea how much it hurt you. I'm not sure they would get it even if you told them in detail upon detail. No, they don't have a clue how much it affected your decisions and relationships. Humbly, but very specifically, forgive them not only for their destructive actions, but also for their *ignorance*. You have no other choice if you want out of that pit.[9]

And that's what we want, yes? Out of the pit. Out of the tomb. Out of the gaping maw of death that would like nothing more than to close its jaws around us and suck us down. However, we were made for life and God wants to give us life—life to the full.

Nothing takes more divine power than forgiveness, and therefore nothing is more powerful than forgiving.[10]

But forgiveness doesn't necessarily imply friendship.

Can you biblically forgive someone without restoring or manufacturing a friendship? Why is this sometimes necessary?

How can forgiving a friend, even without restoration of that friendship, help you with future relationships?

Forgiveness in friendship "does not require condoning some offensive act, forgetting what happened, or reconciling with the perpetrator. It means finding a way to free oneself from the claws of obsession about the hurt."[11] Forgiveness is making peace with the past so that there is opportunity for relationship in the future. Not necessarily with the same people who've scarred us. But sometimes, by the grace of Christ, forgiveness is exactly that powerful to restore broken relationships to fresh health and offer the same people a completely different way of relating to one another.

Forgiveness is the beginning. And it's how we find closure even on the relationships that won't ever be completely restored to us. Because forgiveness is like a pair of tweezers picking out the shards of shrapnel embedded in our hearts and minds by people we once loved. Forgiveness removes the hurt so that we can heal. Forgiveness is the gift we give to ourselves so that we can stop bleeding and begin to grow new skin over old wounds. Forgiveness is the first step out of the dark and into the light.

FRIENDSHIP CHALLENGE

Remember our friendship challenge from Day 1 this week—those hurts we wrote down and that you tucked into your Bible for safekeeping? I want you to find somewhere comfortable to sit. Somewhere you feel safe and won't be interrupted. Take those bits of paper and broken parts of your heart and hold them up in front of you. Tell Jesus what was done to you. Show Him. Let Him see. Read them aloud again if you need to.

You can tell Him it was unfair. He understands unfair from the inside out.

Now close your eyes. And just sit there in the presence of the Holy Spirit. What is Jesus doing? Can you sense His presence? My hope is that you will sense how much He loves you. My hope is that you would be able to imagine that if He was in the room with you, He would be standing up, walking over to you, and taking you in His arms to hug you and comfort you.

My friend, now is the time to shred those bits of paper. Shred them up as small as they can go. With Jesus holding tight onto you, I want you to witness all those words being torn down into little bits and pieces. We can't let them have any power over you anymore. They have no power over your life in Christ because He has come to set you free.

Now, if you have a fireplace or fire pit, burn them. Or you can go one of my favorite routes and flush them down the toilet. Or you can burn them and then flush the ashes. I've done both in the past.

CLOSE BY READING ROMANS 8:31-39.

In the space below write out the verses that comfort you the most from that passage, and receive them as the Holy Spirit speaking wholeness and healing into your most tender and broken places.

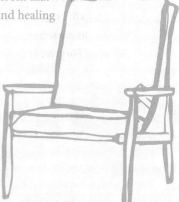

It's not our job to rescue other people. It's our job to love them. It's Jesus' job to rescue them.

FRIENDSHIP TAKES WALKING AWAY WISELY

If possible, as far as it depends on you,
live at peace with everyone.

ROMANS 12:18

FRIENDSHIP ~~takes~~ WALKING AWAY ~~wisely~~

VIEWER GUIDE: SESSION 6

Watch the Session 6 video and discuss with your group the following questions:

1. Deidra shared the story about her "lists." Can you relate? What are other methods we use to "punish" others when they've hurt us?

2. How is having boundaries in a relationship healthy?

3. What can happen when we don't have boundaries?

4. How can you be a friend to someone without necessarily taking on their burdens?

5. Share with your group about an experience when the Holy Spirit prompted you to walk away from a friendship or situation.

6. Lisa-Jo mentions the "disease of politeness." How have you seen this play out in your own friendships?

7. How can stepping out of the way lead to transformation in someone's life?

8. With your group, highlight any meaningful truths you took away from today's conversation at the table.

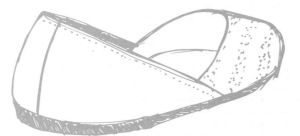

Video sessions available for purchase at *LifeWay.com/WeSavedYouASeat*

IT'S NOT YOUR JOB TO RESCUE OTHER PEOPLE.

One of my favorite cousins lives in South Africa. She has been like a surrogate mom to me over the years and her husband is a doctor. Several years ago he suffered an accidental needle prick. It comes with the territory in the medical field. But for a long, terrible while he didn't know if he had been infected with a virus or not.

It was a hard load to live under.

They didn't tell their kids the source of their worry. But children internalize their parents' anxiety. And their small frames and hearts got heavier and more stooped over under the weight of the worry they could feel in their house. They kept trying to carry it with their small hands and positive attitudes and big eyes, wanting to ask questions they were afraid to hear answers to. They could tell their parents were struggling with an unspoken fear and the littles kept breathing in that air of anxiety until it became part of their own DNA and they adopted that unspoken worry like it was their own. And of course, it almost crushed their tiny frames.

So my cousin and her husband intervened. One night after supper they lined up all three children (at the time aged six and under). A game of pretend was initiated and each kid was given their school backpack to put on. And their parents followed them around the house and yard slowly, methodically adding rocks to the backpacks.

Big, hard, heavy stones. They kept filling the backpacks with those rocks.

At first the children enjoyed the challenge. They could do it. They could still run and play with the heavy packs. But rock after rock had them slowing down. Until all three were at a standstill and the game had lost its fun.

"We can't do this, dad," said their oldest daughter.
"Why? Why can't you?" her father pushed back.
"Because they're too heavy. We're just kids; they're too heavy for us."

Tired, worried eyes looked out from scrunched up faces at their parents. And the parents? They did what parents do. They began unpacking their children's anxieties.

They acknowledged the ominous dread that had entered the house and that the kids had taken to carrying upon themselves. They slowly and clearly explained that this worry was not a weight designed for children. That it was too heavy for them. That managing it or carrying it or even trying to balance it was not up to them. They were not required to bear their parents' fears.

And with that they reached into the backpacks that had been dragging down three sets of small shoulders and began to unpack them. They removed each of those heavy, hard rocks and hurled them into the back garden. The children got in on the spirit of the thing. Satchel straps slipped off small arms. Eager hands grabbed at ugly burdens and threw them far away.

Until those kids were free of the baggage that never belonged to them in the first place.

Sometimes friendship can feel like that. Sometimes, without even realizing we're doing it, we start accumulating the heavy rocks and sharp pieces of broken glass that our friends have been carrying and we put them into our own backpacks. We stuff ourselves full of our friends' hurts and frustrations and heavy, difficult stories and then we wonder why it's so hard to keep walking forward.

> Can you think of a friendship where you collected and carried the broken rocks and sharp glass pieces that didn't really belong to you? Describe what that looked and felt like.

Here's where it gets tricky. As Christians we're taught that it's a good thing to be willing to "Bear one another's burdens, and so fulfill the law of Christ" (Gal. 6:2, ESV). But, if we aren't careful, that can guilt us into putting up with a lot of behavior that is harmful to us. Because being willing to "bear one another's burdens" is not the same as being willing to bear one another's dysfunction, rage, inappropriate behavior, manipulation, passive aggression, cruelty, control, and a whole host of other traits that we can inhale like secondhand smoke in some friendships without even being aware of it.

But when we spend some time with those first verses in Galatians 6 we discover that the challenge to "bear one another's burdens" is in fact a call to hold one another accountable for our "moral burdens or weaknesses."[1] It is not an excuse to enable those behaviors. See for yourself, what does the verse just before verse 2 say?

Write out Galatians 6:1.

The NIV Study Bible notes point out that the Greek word for the verb *restore* used in verse 1 is used elsewhere in the New Testament to refer to "mending nets (Mark 1:19) and bringing factions together (1 Cor. 1:10)."[2] This is about assistance, not about transference. This is about friendship motivated by faithfulness, not manipulated by guilt.

Let's look at the instructions for healthy relationships in Galatians 6:1-5. I think that they can be summed up in three strong calls to action: Verse 1: Mend. Verse 2: Carry. And Verses 3-5: Attend. Let's unpack that a bit.

> [1] Brothers and sisters, if someone is overtaken in any wrongdoing, you who are spiritual, restore such a person with a gentle spirit, watching out for yourselves so that you also won't be tempted. [2] Carry one another's burdens; in this way you will fulfill the law of Christ. [3] For if anyone considers himself to be something when he is nothing, he deceives himself. [4] Let each person examine his own work, and then he can take pride in himself alone, and not compare himself with someone else. [5] For each person will have to carry his own load.
> GALATIANS 6:1-5

VERSE 1: MEND

The challenge is to restore or mend a friend so that she finds her way back toward better choices—back toward Christ.

Underline the words in verse 1 that illustrate this challenge.

Now write down what that might look like in real life for you and your friends.

VERSE 2: CARRY

The second challenge is to carry a friend's burdens. The HCSB Study Bible describes these as their "physical, emotional or spiritual load" that's threatening to crush them.[3]

Underline the words in verse two that illustrate that challenge.

Now, note how the charge to "mend a friend" comes before the charge to "carry a friend's burdens." This is important. Why do you think?

This order is important because it helps us keep our obligations straight. Instead of being guilted into making excuses for a friend's bad behavior, we're called to first be an agent of change in her life and help mend bad behavior before we help offer broad and sympathetic shoulders as she works her way out from under that burden. We are called to be agents of change. We are not called to enable bad behavior. And we are definitely not called to adopt their bad behavior as our own. Remember what the second part of verse 1 said.

VERSES 3-5: ATTEND

The challenge in these verses is to attend to your own load without comparing, condescending, or controlling.

Underline the words in verses 3-5 that illustrate that challenge.

Note, the Greek word used here for "load" is not the same word used in verse 2 for "burdens." Instead, in this verse the word means the "cargo" or "capacity" that we've been assigned by the Lord.[4] While mending and attending to our friends we can't become distracted from the responsibility of carrying our own loads—the specific callings, challenges, or tests that Christ has entrusted to us. We don't trade one in for the other. Instead, we remain faithful to both.

So, why do these three challenges (and the order they appear in) to mend, carry, and attend matter so much?

I think they matter because we're not always good at getting the order or the actions right. As Christian women I think we are particularly susceptible to the "disease of politeness." It can be deadly. It can cause us to make excuses instead of take action. Even when we're neck deep in a relationship that's starting to throttle us because we've exchanged the loads God has entrusted us with for the baggage friends have guilted us with.

Sometimes it is simply hope that a person will change that keeps us carrying our friends' baggage. There might be very few things more painful than a hope that disappoints. And it's the reason we often end up shouldering the burdens of our friends, instead of helping them carry those burdens themselves. Because we so badly want to see them healthy and fulfilled. Sometimes we're more invested in their well-being than they are.

In their book, *Safe People*, Drs. Cloud and Townsend unpack what hopeful creatures we humans are and how it's that very optimism that can keep us making excuses or hoping for change. And instead of helping mend we've started to bend to accommodate the behaviors of friends beyond the point of healthy interactions:

> *Humans are incredible optimists when it comes to destructive relationships. For some reason we think that a person who is hurtful, irresponsible, out of control, abusive, or dishonest is going to change if we just love them correctly or more or enough. We think that if we just let them know about their mistakes, or cry the blues, or get angry, that they will change. ... In this scenario we use hope to defend ourselves against facing the truth about someone we love. We do not want to go through the sadness of realizing that they probably are not going to change. We don't want to accept the reality about who they are. So, we hope.*[5]

So what then? What if we have tried all three steps—mending, carrying, and attending—and nothing has changed? How do we love well without being dragged down by the weight of a friendship that's become too heavy and too unhealthy to keep carrying? How do we figure out when to keep trying and when it might be beyond our ability to fix things?

We'll unpack those answers over the next two days. For today it's important to simply make sure we understand what God has required of us and to keep in mind that it's not our job to rescue other people; it's our job to love them. It's Jesus' job to rescue them.

FRIENDSHIP CHALLENGE

Are you carrying around someone else's broken bits and pieces in your backpack? Has it started to feel too heavy? Is it starting to cause you resentment, bitterness, or panic? Can you be really honest and write down the things you think you might have taken on that were never yours to carry in the first place?

_____

_____

_____

_____

_____

_____

Now, identify your own mend, carry, attend journey. Can you chart it below so that you know where you currently are in relation to that friendship?

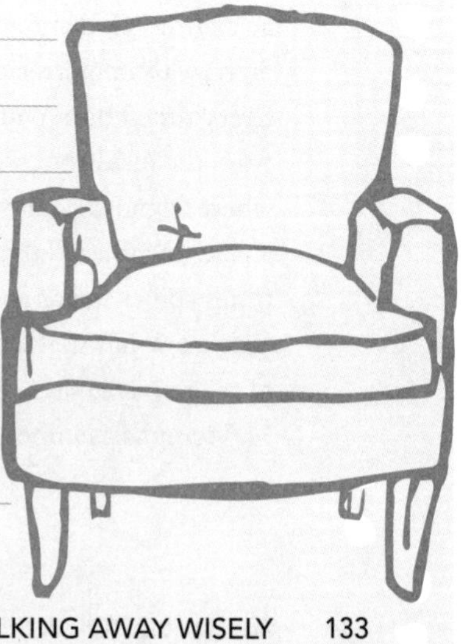

_____

_____

_____

_____

_____

_____

_____

_____

_____

_____

_____

_____

_____

DAY 2

FEAR GOD NOT PEOPLE.

If ever there was a handbook on how to negotiate hard relationships and create fresh starts it's the Bible: "The chief theme of the entire Bible is reconciliation of unsafe relationships."[6] First, between us and God. And second between us and the other people God has created. All throughout Scripture we see how God is relentless in His quest to remake us in His own image, often through our relationships with other people—even the hard relationships. Sometimes especially through those difficult ones.

Because God is in the business of doing what according to Revelation 21:5?

This is what He modeled in his own relationships. He didn't give up on the hard, difficult frustrating ones. Instead, He facilitated healing. We see Him do this with Adam and Eve, Cain, Noah, Moses, Joshua, Rahab, David, Ruth, Peter, Paul, and on and on down through history to the bickering disciples, the early church, and all the way on to you and me and that coworker or PTA parent who makes you grind your teeth in irritation. God wants wholeness. God wants health. He wants unbroken relationships with Him forever.

Things obviously didn't work out that way: "People turned toward self-centeredness and away from God and his ways. And God was faced with the same dilemma that we are faced with in our relationships in a fallen world: Do I keep them, or do I move on?"[7] Every time I bump into another real time, real life example that God understands my life from the inside out, I'm surprised all over again. That He understands my tender scabs where friendships have cut and where I haven't been able to put things back together again. I'm amazed that the God of the universe and I share the same aching cry that sometimes comes out as a whimper and sometimes as a gut cry of confusion, "I have been *hurt*" (Ezek. 6:9, NASB; emphasis mine). And in the HCSB the word used is *crushed*—the God of the universe says, "I was *crushed* by their promiscuous hearts that turned away from Me" (emphasis mine).

God gets it. From the inside out He knows what a betrayal by a friend feels like. And His pain can be heard loudly from the pages of both the Old and the New Testaments. If He's our role model in His hurt then He can also be trusted as our role model in how to respond. And it's not what you might think. It's not a quick kick to the curb. No, instead God lives up to His own Word and His character.

Write down God's defining character traits as listed in 1 Corinthians 13:4-7:

Nothing will require us to put these into practice like relationships with other people. Indeed, you wouldn't need this list if you were the only human being on the planet. This is a checklist for how to thrive alongside other human beings. Drs. Cloud and Townsend who authored, *Safe People,* extrapolate from this list what God's consistent response to hurt has been throughout Scriptures, down through history and into our own lives today:

WE FIND THAT GOD

1. STARTS FROM A LOVED POSITION,

2. ACTS RIGHTEOUSLY,

3. USES THE COMMUNITY TO TRANSFORM,

4. ACCEPTS REALITY AND FORGIVES,

5. GIVES CHANGE A CHANCE, AND

6. IS LONG-SUFFERING.[8]

This list is not what I want to hear when I'm worn down by a difficult relationship. Instead, when I've done all that I believe I can, I have been known to tell God, "Well, I'm done." As I metaphorically dust off my hands and pat myself on the back for giving it such a good go. And I believe it. I'm done being patient and done trying to stand in her shoes and done trying to keep my heart open and done keeping my passive aggression in check and done with second, third, fourth chances.

And I believe I'm justified in feeling that way because just look, God! Look at all my hard work. Look at how I've cried and wrestled and felt horrible and gone back and tried again.

And look where we *still* are. Obviously this has to be the end, yes? I mean, at some point we run out of trying. We run out of do-overs. We run out of interest or patience or conversations. At some point, surely, we both just get to be done.

But God, I have found, is stubborn. And He has stubbornly insisted in my life that there is no "done" when it comes to sacrificial love. There is only "more." This has been a shocking revelation to me. Shocking and, frankly, unwelcome. To discover that more would be expected of me. More listening. More changing. More bending. More willingness to be open. More awkward and more choosing to stay instead of cutting loose and quitting. God has kept me in some relationships way, uncomfortably beyond what I would have considered to be the finish line.

But He hasn't left me there alone. He's always been intimately involved and insanely patient with me. And it has changed me. That's the kicker. It has changed me when I thought it was about changing the other person. It has taken apart all my assumptions about love and kindness and patience and that old-school word "long-suffering" and put them back together again in a picture that demonstrates how eternal God's patience is with me. With all of us.

> Look up the definition of *long-suffering* and write it below.

I have found Him rabid in His ability to out-wait our selfishness, our stubbornness, our insistence on doing things our own way. He has walked me down the winding corridors of "more" miles and miles further than I ever would have thought my legs or my heart could take. There will be some relationships that are so poisoned and bitter that we need to stop letting them feed us; we need to cut the ties and walk away so that we can live. So that both of us can live. So that we can thrive in our individual lanes and keep running hard for the kingdom. And we'll talk more about those tomorrow.

But there are other friendships that are assignments straight from Jesus Himself. That He's using to get up in your business and teach you some things about yourself. Some friendships where He's asking you to actually be His patience and grace and compassion personified in actual arms and time and conversations. Friendships where there isn't a shortcut to cutting out the tension that seems to have grown up out of nowhere between you. Being human comes with other human beings so if we stop, drop, and cut them off any time we're offended, annoyed, frustrated, or unable to make sense of the current state of the friendship, we will soon enough find ourselves friendless and alone.

Yesterday, I sat down at my desk and made a list of the things I've lost because of friendships. Because of friends who have challenged me, pushed me out of my comfort zone, and forced me to look up from the solar system of my own creation where I've so regularly assumed I was the sun. The truth of it is that those friendships, the ones that have rubbed me raw as they've reminded me that I am not the center of the universe, have given me the gift of *subtraction*. We're so one-track minded when it comes to friendship, so programmed to look for what's in it for me, that sometimes we forget the best thing we can get out of a friendship might be one of the things we have lost because of it.

My hardest friendships have cost me. The love and patience they've required have cost me huge chunks of my pride. I've lost parts of my arrogance along the way and my inability to see the world from someone else's perspective. I've lost my unwillingness to compromise and I've had to give up my stubborn refusal to apologize.

Some friendships are like a meat tenderizer. And sometimes that is what our hearts require. Our puffed up, stubborn, arrogant hearts sometimes need the pounding, tenderizing mercy of a God who wants us to be malleable, capable of profound compassion, and quick to give someone else the benefit of the doubt. Being willing to let God work in me and through me for the sake of healing what was once a deeply unhealthy friendship has been nothing short of miraculous.

But it's required a focus on Him instead of my default of stewing and obsessing about how I'm being treated by a friend. It has required paying attention to what God wants, not what my friend or I want. It has required not letting my feelings be the boss of me. Instead, it's been about recognizing that if a friendship has any hope of surviving I need to let the Holy Spirit be the boss of me. Because where we go for wisdom in these hard friendship moments is essential.

MY OWN GUT OR TEMPER OR SELF-PITY IS A TERRIBLE PLACE TO LOOK FOR WISDOM. INSTEAD, LET'S READ PSALM 111:10 AND PROVERBS 9:10.

In both of these passages, what is described as the beginning or the foundation of wisdom?

Jesus was constantly loving beyond the borders of what we can ever begin to imagine. His love was lavish, unafraid, and extravagant. He opened His heart and His life to the people who loved Him back as well as to those who spit in His face. That kind of love will wrench you. It will wring you out. It will require more of you than you thought possible. But it will drive you deep into Jesus' side until His feelings become your feelings and together you might just find a miracle—the dry bones of a dead friendship coming back to life.

In Oswald Chambers' words, "It is impossible to exhaust God's love, and it is impossible to exhaust my love if it flows from the Spirit of God within me."[9] We can always borrow God's feelings for our friends when we're struggling with our own. He promises to pour Himself out into us and then through us, and the only thing we have to do is bring willingness to the equation. We have to be willing to receive His patience, kindness, long-suffering nature, and love and then be willing to pass it on to our friends.

I like to think, man I need to believe, that those rough edges of my younger self are slowly being sanded away by friends who've lived alongside me and rubbed off on me with their own generous grace where none was deserved. So that when those bumpy days arrive and you start to doubt your friends and it becomes hard to keep believing the best about them, I remember that sometimes the best work God does inside our souls is the most uncomfortable.

So on those days, on the days I am struggling to feel love, grace, compassion, or patience toward other humans, I ask God if I can borrow His feelings. If I can swap all my frustration for a slice of His worldview and a chunk of His feelings toward my fellow womankind. This is the God who has loved them deeper and longer and who knows their rough edges and hurt insides better than we ever will. And this is the God who generously pours out His love and who never runs out and who is defined by compassion and speaks in grace and walked the walk all the way to the cross and down into the dark tomb and out into the light again. With access to that kind of love, my own tired heart can be resurrected and keep opening up to keep loving while buried deeply and safely inside the shield of His own.

> For it is God who is working in you both to will [feel/want] and to work [act] according to his good purpose.
> PHILIPPIANS 2:13

God will supply you with what you need. He will work in, through, and for you so that you can be a blessing to the women around you instead of letting Satan explode a relationship that Jesus wants to put back together.

FRIENDSHIP CHALLENGE

What are the things that you've lost because of friendships? The things you needed to lose? Spend some time thinking back on challenging friendships that have helped you mature. What have they helped you lose?

_____

_____

_____

_____

_____

_____

_____

Now, when you think about challenging friendships, does someone specific come to mind? Is there a woman who is rubbing you the wrong way? Instead of giving into your irritation with her, let's spend some time today asking God what He might be trying to teach you through that friendship. What does He want you to lose to make room for more of Him? Pray, open your heart, and then write down what comes to mind.

_____

_____

_____

_____

_____

_____

_____

WALK AWAY WISELY

The reality of friendship is that we live in a broken world—a world broken by sin—and we feel the consequences of that daily. We serve a King who has given His life to redeem this broken world and to put it back together. He is at work in the world building His kingdom and making stained-glass art out of all the sharp and shattered pieces of our lives. But in the midst of that process He has been up front and told us that we "will have suffering in this world" (John 16:33). This world *will* break our hearts the way it broke His. And while He has overcome the world, if we follow in His footsteps we will share in His scars.

Jesus left this world with scars on His hands, feet, and side, and I'm certain they criss-crossed deep, painful grooves into His heart. So if your own heart aches, then know you are not alone. You are living the legacy of the God who came to show us the way, the God who rode into Jerusalem weeping for the people and the city who would betray Him and themselves. But that didn't slow Him down or stop Him from coming to them, from coming to us.

So when a friendship has broken into bits and pieces too painful for us to keep carrying, then in my experience we can offer them back to Jesus. **Leaning deep into Jesus' sacrificial love will walk you much deeper and longer into opening up your heart to love people you never thought you could love** until either the friendship is healed or you recognize that it's beyond your ability to raise it from the dead; you can't carry that burden anymore.

Then, friend, I believe that Jesus will lift the burden off you. But here's what makes Him the very definition of love: He won't discard that friend. No, I believe He will take the burden onto His own shoulders and into His own heart—the place where it has lived all along—and He will keep carrying it Himself. He will free you to walk alongside Him as He carries all that hurt and pain all the way with Him up onto the cross and down into the grave and back out into the light again. **While darkness might try to blot out a friendship, Jesus is the Light of the world.**

In him was life, and that life was the light of men. That light shines in the darkness, and yet the darkness did not overcome it.
JOHN 1:4-5

What do these verses say about the attempt by darkness to blot out Christ's light?

It is not for us to judge the hearts of our friends. It's for us to keep following Jesus. In some friendships that will mean following Him as He walks us away from a friend. Those relationships riddled with so much hurt and so many unhealthy habits that, instead of growing us both toward God, grew us away—like poison ivy that would choke the life out of the trees it wraps itself around and sting anyone who tries to remove it.

In order to be agents of peace, of long-suffering, of long walks with a God who doesn't turn His back on relationship, we need to be healthy ourselves. Every time a relationship has been more toxic than I could possibly transform, I was either too young or too vulnerable or too unqualified to be able to make anything healthy out of that environment. Some wounds need professional, tender counseling from those qualified to speak objectively into a raw and hurting person. In those cases, God has given me the protection of being able to grant forgiveness while simultaneously opening an exit for me to leave so there was still a chance to heal separately. Forgiveness does not negate consequence, and change has to be chosen; it can't be forced.

I remember the afternoon that God released me from a friendship I couldn't seem to save. I was driving our old, red pickup truck at the end of a hot, sticky day. The windows were down because the air conditioning wasn't working. I was driving to get burgers and fries for the kids for dinner. As usual I was pretzeling my mind into knots to try to make sense of how to keep walking forward in a friendship that seemed to keep moving backward. I was so tired, but I was more determined than I'd ever been to love far beyond my borders. To love in a way that didn't make sense to me. To love even when I didn't understand if anything good was coming out of that loving.

As I passed a small chapel on the right side of the road and pulled into the fast-food parking lot, I felt a weight shift off my heart. It seemed that the Holy Spirit had said two words to me: "You're done." Just like that. In the moment I knew it was true. The task He'd sent me was over. I won't know until I meet God face-to-face if I walked as far and true and deeply into the call of love He'd set before me as He wanted me to or not. I won't know if my attempt came close to what He was asking of me. But today I know that I no longer carry that load. Instead, He's taken it onto His wide, trustworthy shoulders and let me walk out from under the burden.

> Can you describe a time when you felt released from a situation like mine? A friendship that you were no longer required to try to fix?

But we release those burdens and walk away from those friendships slowly, without slamming and bolting the door behind us. Because we believe in a God who raises hopeless, dead bones back to life. With my hope firmly placed in Him I want that door unlocked so that friendship has a chance for resurrection. But until then I know I can trust Him with it, because our God of *shalom* doesn't just want wholeness. He is wholeness. He is "the way, the truth, and the life" (John 14:6), moving all of humanity toward right relationship with Him and with each other *through* Him.

I've heard versions of this same story told over plates of pizza and across a farmhouse table over shared chips and salsa. One friend said she thought it had been goodbye. She thought there wouldn't be room for restoration, but she never stopped praying. Four years later the shut door of a dear friendship creaked its way back open again.

Another wise woman told the story of fifteen years spent interceding for a brutally diffi-cult relationship at work. Transfer or resignation would have been her preference, but God kept her praying and at times begging Him for health, for life, and for hope in this broken relationship. "Those are the kinds of prayers," she told me, "that God loves to answer." Fifteen years later and the evening she told us the story she'd just come home from the funeral of her colleague's son. A funeral she still couldn't believe she'd been invited to attend—with the woman she's since held in her arms as they wept together. The woman who spent years refusing to talk to her.

Jesus and Paul often said that we sometimes have to leave someone, that some relationships have to end.[10]

Let's look at a few examples.

WRITE DOWN THE RELATIONSHIP THAT ENDED IN THESE PASSAGES AND WHY:

Matthew 18:15-17   Titus 3:10

There are also examples of relationships being restored in the stories that the Bible preserved for us.

READ HOW PAUL AND BARNABAS DISAGREED OVER JOHN MARK, BUT THEN HOW LATER PAUL WOULD TAKE MARK WITH HIM:

After some time had passed, Paul said to Barnabas, "Let's go back and visit the brothers and sisters in every town where we have preached the word of the Lord and see how they're doing." Barnabas wanted to take along John Mark. But Paul insisted that they should not take along this man who had deserted them in Pamphylia and had not gone on with them to the work. They had such a sharp disagreement that they parted company, and Barnabas took Mark with him and sailed off to Cyprus. But Paul chose Silas and departed, after being commended by the brothers and sisters to the grace of the Lord.
ACTS 15:36-40

Why didn't Paul want to take Mark with them?

What kind of disagreement did Paul and Barnabas have?

Aristarchus, my fellow prisoner, sends you greetings, as does Mark, Barnabas's cousin (concerning whom you have received instructions: if he comes to you, welcome him).
COLOSSIANS 4:10

What was Mark's relationship to Barnabas?

What sentence tells us Mark was with Paul?

How did Paul say that the church in Colossae should treat Mark?

While sometimes separation is necessary, the hope is always that it isn't permanent. Part of what Jesus' brother, James, described as "the hard work of getting along" (Jas. 3:18, MSG) in community includes being willing to address inappropriate behavior and set appropriate boundaries with consequences.

I have learned that forgiveness doesn't require friendship in order to be genuine. Forgiveness does not equal allowing unsafe people into our safe, inner circles. "Boundaries are our spiritual and emotional 'property lines.' They tell us where we end, and where others begin. They help to keep good things in us, and bad things out. We take responsibility for what is ours, and not for what isn't. When [our boundaries] are clearly defined, we can carry our own loads, and we know when it's appropriate to help others with their burdens (Gal. 6:1-5)."[11]

Drawing safe boundary lines doesn't make you selfish, unChristian, or impolite. It makes you wise. And it puts our hope in the right place—in the Christ who can actually transform us and "will not disappoint us" (Rom. 5:5) instead of in our friends who can't help but fail us, because like us, they're human and flawed. Safe boundary lines and housing your hope in the right place will make you all the more capable of being a woman who is a safe place for her friends to unload their heavy burdens and trust that they will find encouragement in the shade of your friendship without codependency or guilt.

Whether we like it or not, we all haul some kind of baggage with us into our adult friendships. And we all need to be reminded that we're not responsible for the luggage that other women will bring with them. Yet we will be impacted by it and should be ready for when those suitcases of junk inevitably explode at inconvenient times when all you thought you were doing was making plans for lunch and instead you end up down a dark and twisting conversation you never expected.

Take a minute to reflect on the last few paragraphs. When have you needed to put boundaries in place for the sake of yourself or your friendship?

What baggage have you carried into a friendship? How have others responded to your baggage?

Jesus-type friendship is about taking Romans 12:18 literally when it says, "If it is possible, as far as it depends on you, live at peace with everyone" (NIV). We only know if it is possible if we have done all we can. If we have followed in Christ's footsteps and behaved in a way that honors our friend and our Savior. That checklist for living at peace with everyone, as far as it depends on you, might look something like the way God responds to hurt, as we identified in day 2 from *Safe People*. God ...

- □ **"STARTS FROM A LOVED POSITION,"** so I will approach this relationship from the security of my identity in Christ, rejecting codependency, and believing that in Christ I am loved, chosen, and cherished (John 3:16).
- □ **"ACTS RIGHTEOUSLY,"** so I take responsibility for how my own behavior may have impacted the friendship. I will work to change, ask forgiveness where necessary, and move toward health (Matt. 7:1-5). I am not simply returning "evil for evil" (Rom. 12:17).
- □ **"USES THE COMMUNITY TO TRANSFORM,"** so I will be honest with friends who know us both, ask for their advice, and be open to learn and change and grow from it (Prov. 11:14).
- □ **"ACCEPTS REALITY AND FORGIVES,"** so I won't try to twist my friend into my own image. I have accepted her as she is, uniquely created in God's image. And where she has hurt me, I have not held a grudge. I can honestly say that I have freely forgiven her as Christ forgave me (Eph. 4:32).
- □ **"GIVES CHANGE A CHANCE,"** so I won't quit when the friendship gets tough. I will stay. I will love and forgive. I will let God change me where I need it. And I am open to seeing the friendship grow and change (Matt. 18:21-22).
- □ **"IS LONG-SUFFERING."** So I will practice patience. I will not give up on this friendship easily. When God has asked me to, I will go the extra mile with my whole heart (Ex. 34:6-7).[12]

Go back and read through the list above. Check any areas you are working through in your own current friendships.

When we have faithfully and honestly done these things, then we can know that we are women who are safe places for friendship. We are women undaunted by the hard or heavy stories our friends bring with them into our friendships. But we are also women who can be released from the false guilt we so often feel at the thought of walking away from an unhealthy friendship—a friendship that as far as it is possible, *as far as it depends on you,* you haven't been able to fix.

Giving ourselves permission to forgive the hurt of a friendship and still walk away from it is a necessary life skill. *But emphasis on the walk.* This isn't about running away from friends, quitting friendships, or ruthlessly cutting inconvenient friends out of your life. This is about becoming healthy people for the sake of ourselves and our friends, and sometimes that requires distance.

Leaving a friendship will come with sadness. Jesus was called "a man of sorrows" (Isa. 53:3, ESV), and those of us who follow Him won't be immune from His grief. When we walk away from a destructive relationship, there's a loss and sadness. If we do not face the loss, and the sadness with it, we can find ourselves going back to the same relationship or another destructive one like it.[13]

We worship a God who is defined by His passion to make "everything new" (Rev. 21:5), and Christ makes all things new (2 Cor. 5:17)—even (and maybe especially) friendships between His daughters. In the meantime, He invites us to wield the power of praise. Let's end our time this week by reading the staggering story of King Jehoshaphat and how He overcame terrible odds by the power of praising the Lord.

READ 2 CHRONICLES 20:14-26.

The valley where God handed them the victory was named the Valley of Beracah. Why? What does that mean according to verse 26?

In the face of lost friendships and scarred hearts, there might be nothing as unexpected or as powerful as refusing to sink under the sea of false guilt or sadness but instead throwing out our arms as we lean into a life of praising the God who is the Giver of all good gifts, especially the gift of friendship. This moment right now that aches, this moment that comes with scars, it might be the moment you remember as your Valley of Praise.

So, sisters, stand firm, keep focused on what God has asked you to do, and wield the power of praise over every aspect of your friendships. Especially today.

FRIENDSHIP CHALLENGE

READ FROM JAMES 3. MY FAVORITE VERSION IS IN THE MESSAGE TRANSLATION:

Real wisdom, God's wisdom, begins with a holy life and is characterized by getting along with others. It is gentle and reasonable, overflowing with mercy and blessings, not hot one day and cold the next, not two-faced. You can develop a healthy, robust community that lives right with God and enjoy its results *only* if you do the hard work of getting along with each other, treating each other with dignity and honor.
JAMES 3:17-18, MSG

Write down each aspect of healthy friendship highlighted by this passage.
Then ask yourself three final questions:

1. Am I honestly doing "the hard work of getting along with" my friends? How?

2. If not, what should I start doing differently? Or if I already am, what can I practice doing better? Be very specific in your answers. Here is your chance to challenge yourself and to go deeper in your friendships.

3. Have I embraced the power of praise in my life? Let's end our time together with a prayer of praise to our God who is the very definition of friendship. Let's thank Him for the gift, example, and challenge of His friendship. Amen and amen.

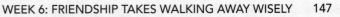

FRIENDSHIP

isn't something we passively receive. Friendship is something we actively do.

WEEK 7:
FRIENDSHIP TAKES ACTION

"Which of these three do you think proved to be a neighbor
to the man who fell into the hands of the robbers?"
"The one who showed mercy to him," he said.
Then Jesus told him, "Go and do the same."

LUKE 10:36-37

Friendship TAKES action

VIEWER GUIDE: SESSION 7

Watch the Session 7 video and discuss with your group the following questions:

1. Describe a time when you "dared to go first."

2. Read the parable of the good Samaritan in Luke 10:25-37. Lisa-Jo noted that this parable teaches us how to be a good neighbor. Describe some of the ways we can be a good neighbor from this parable.

3. How can being on the receiving end of friendship sometimes be difficult for us?

4. Alia talked about being surprised by friendships. How has God surprised you with the friendships in your life?

5. How has God used other people to bring change or transformation in your life?

6. How have you seen friendship do the work of the body of Christ?

7. Describe how you have seen the need for friendship embedded into our spiritual DNA.

8. How do we see Christ's love for us through our friendships with others?

9. With your group, highlight any meaningful truths you took away from today's conversation at the table.

Video sessions available for purchase at *LifeWay.com/WeSavedYouASeat*

Leader GUIDE

We Saved You a Seat is a video and discussion based Bible study. The weekly homework along with the teaching videos will promote honest conversation as you study Scripture together. Conversation is essential to the experience, so I've provided some review or starter questions. After your group has time to get settled and review the previous week's work, join the (in)courage ladies at the table for that session's video. Use the provided discussion questions afterward to learn from each other.

TIPS ON LEADING THIS BIBLE STUDY

PRAY. As you prepare to lead *We Saved You a Seat,* remember that prayer is essential. Set aside time each week to pray for the women in your group. Listen to their needs and the struggles they're facing so you can bring them before the Lord. Though organizing and planning are important, protect your time of prayer before each gathering. Encourage your women to include prayer as part of their own daily spiritual discipline as well.

GUIDE. Accept women where they are but also set expectations that motivate commitment. Be consistent and trustworthy. Encourage women to follow through on the study, attend the group sessions, and engage with the homework. Listen carefully,

responsibly guide discussion, and keep confidences shared within the group. Be honest and vulnerable by sharing what God is teaching you throughout the study. Most women will follow your lead and be more willing to share and participate when they see your transparency. Reach out to different ages, backgrounds, and stages of life. This is sure to make your conversation and experience richer.

CONNECT. Stay engaged with the women. Use social media, emails, or a quick note in the mail to connect with the group and share prayer needs throughout the week. Let them know when you are praying specifically for them. Root everything in Scripture and encourage them in their relationship with Jesus.

CELEBRATE. At the end of the study, celebrate what God has done by having your group share what they've learned and how they've grown. Pray together about what commitment God is asking from them as a result of this study.

TIPS ON ORGANIZING THIS BIBLE STUDY

TALK TO YOUR PASTOR OR ADMINISTRATOR. If you're leading this as part of a local church, ask for their input, prayers, and support.

SECURE YOUR LOCATION. Think about the number of women you can accommodate in the designated location. Reserve any tables, chairs, or media equipment for the videos and additional audio needs.

PROVIDE CHILDCARE. If you are targeting moms of young children and/or single moms, this is essential.

PROVIDE RESOURCES. Order leader kits and the needed number of Bible study books. You might get a few extra for last minute sign-ups.

PLAN AND PREPARE. Become familiar with the Bible study resource and leader helps available. Preview the video session and prepare the outline you will follow to lead the group meeting based on the leader helps available. Go to *LifeWay.com/WeSavedYouASeat* to find free extra leader and promotional resources for your study.

EVALUATE. After each group session ask, *What went well? What could be improved? Did you see women's lives transformed? Did your group grow closer to Christ and to one another?*

NEXT STEPS. Even after the study concludes, follow up and challenge women to stay involved with others through another Bible study, church opportunity, or anything that will continue their spiritual growth and friendships. Provide several options of ministry opportunities the members can participate in individually or as a group to apply what they have learned through this study.

SESSION 1

The following suggestions will supplement the discussion starter questions on the viewer guide pages. They are intended to assist you and stimulate discussion.

1. Ask "get to know you" questions: Where are you from? What do you do? Are you married? Do you have children?

2. What drew you to participating in a Bible study about friendship?

3. Describe a good friend.

4. Do you consider yourself a good friend? Why or why not?

5. What do you hope to gain from this study and the time spent together?

SESSION 2

For Sessions 2-7 consider beginning each week with an invitation to group members to share from their personal study by asking the first question below.

1. Would anyone care to share any experiences from your friendship challenges this week?

2. How did you answer the prompts on pages 12-13: When I think about friendship, I feel, remember, wish ...

3. When you hear the words *protected* and *guarded* what do they bring to mind? (p. 17)

4. How did you complete the following sentences on page 21: I'm worried if I tell people how I'm really doing they will feel …

5. If someone else shared how she was really doing, instead of just saying she was "fine," I'd feel …

6. Describe a reaction you've had to someone else's sorrow or joy. (p. 28)

SESSION 3

1. Would anyone care to share any experiences from your friendship challenges this week?

2. When have you felt like God has let you down? (p. 39)

3. Discuss the relationship between Jesus and the sisters, Mary and Martha. Did you learn something new about their relationship? Do you feel that you can approach Jesus with such honesty? Why or why not?

4. How do you respond to the quote on page 42: "Ours is a God we can vent to, ours is a God who will cry with us, but most crucial—ours is a God who will raise our deepest hurts from the dead because He is just as angry as we are at what sin steals from us"?

5. How did you complete the sentence on page 44: "I want people to think that I am _____ because I'm afraid they won't like me if they discover I am actually _____"?

6. Who are the everyday people you feel most comfortable with? Why is it easier to feel comfortable with them over others?

SESSION 4

1. Would anyone care to share any experiences from your friendship challenges this week?

2. What kind of person did you write down as the focus of your own unexpected comparison moment? What were some of the feelings stirred within you? (p. 60)

3. How do you complete this phrase from page 60: I've been comparing myself to _____ because _____?

4. Name a few things that you're thankful for on your list from page 75.

5. How easy is it for you to get pulled into the comparison game? What are things you tend to compare to others?

6. Jonathan and David had a unique friendship. How can you affirm God's calling on your friends' lives without envy or jealousy?

SESSION 5

1. Would anyone care to share any experiences from your friendship challenges this week?

2. How did you answer the questions on page 85: Can you put into your own words what you think James and John were really

asking for in this passage, and why? Have you ever done something similar? When?

3. How have you found yourself looking for a seat at "the cool kids" table?

4. What does Jesus' interaction with the brothers, James and John, show us about service?

5. What does your "everyday ministry of the gospel" look like? (pp. 91-92)

6. What did you learn about the word *shalom?* How can we show *shalom* in our friendships?

SESSION 6

1. Would anyone care to share any experiences from your friendship challenges this week?

2. How did you answer the questions on page 104: How have you been hurt by a friend? How do you think it's affected your subsequent friendships?

3. What did you find in your own research about the physical benefits of forgiveness? (p. 119)

4. Describe a situation in which you knew a person haphazardly hurt you. How did you know it was an accident? Were you able to forgive them easily? Why? (p. 119)

5. Can you biblically forgive someone without restoring or manufacturing a friendship? Why is this sometimes necessary? (p. 122)

6. How can forgiving a friend, even without restoration of that friendship, help you with future relationships? (p. 122)

SESSION 7

1. Would anyone care to share any experiences from your friendship challenges this week?

2. Can you think of a friendship where you collected and carried the broken rocks and sharp glass pieces that didn't really belong to you? Describe what that looked and felt like. (p. 129)

3. So why do these three challenges (and the order they appear in) to mend, carry, and attend matter so much? (p. 132)

4. Can you describe a time when you felt released from a situation like mine? A friendship that you were no longer required to try to fix? (p. 142)

5. When have you needed to put boundaries in place for the sake of yourself or your friendship? (p. 144)

6. What baggage have you carried into a friendship? How have others responded to your baggage? (p. 145)

ENDNOTES

Week 1

1. Charles John Ellicott, *Ellicott's Commentary for English Readers* (1905), accessed on March 1, 2017, via *biblehub.com/commentaries/john/17-12.htm*.

2. Joseph Exell and Henry Donald Maurice Spence-Jones, eds., *Pulpit Commentary*, accessed on March 1, 2017, via *http://biblehub.com/commentaries/john/17-12.htm*

3. Dietrich Bonhoeffer, *Life Together: The Classic Exploration of Christian in Community* (New York: Harper & Row, 1954), 99.

4. Merrill C. Tenney and Richard N. Longenecker, *The Expositor's Bible Commentary, Volume 9: John and Acts*, ed. Frank E. Gaebelein (Grand Rapids: Zondervan, 1891), accessed via *mywsb.com*.

5. Ibid.

6. Ibid., John 2:11.

7. Ibid., John 11:14-15.

Week 2

1. Kenneth L. Baker, ed., *NIV Study Bible* (Grand Rapids: Zondervan, 2008), accessed via *mywsb.com*.

2. Edwin A. Blum and Jeremy Royal Howard, ed., *HCSB Study Bible* (Nashville: Holman Bible Publishers, 2010), accessed via *mywsb.com*.

3. Timothy Keller, *The Freedom of Self Forgetfulness: The Path to True Christian Joy*, (Leland, UK: 10Publishing, 2012) 44.

4. "Roman Imperial Theology and the Gospel," York College. Available online at *http://york.edu/fewheel/John/Powerpoints/Roman%20Imperial%20Theology.pdf*.

5. *Zondervan Illustrated Bible Backgrounds Commentary: Matthew, Mark, Luke, Vol. 1*, ed. Clinton E. Arnold (Grand Rapids: Zondervan, 2002), accessed via *mywsb.com*.

6. Rodney A. Whitacre, *The IVP New Testament Commentary Series: John*, accessed via *mywsb.com*.

7. Ibid.

Week 3

1. Priscilla Shirer, *Fervent: A Woman's Battle Plan for Serious, Specific, and Strategic Prayer* (Nashville: B & H Publishing, 2015), 57.

2. Dr. Henry Cloud and Dr. John Townsend, *Safe People: How to Find Relationships That Are Good for You and Avoid Those That Aren't* (Grand Rapids: Zondervan, 2005), Kindle location 935.

3. Dr. Dan B. Allender and Dr. Tremper Longman III, *Bold Love* (Colorado Springs: NavPress, 1992), 291.

4. Timothy Keller, "Adoration: Hallowed Be Thy Name," *Gospel in Life*, April 30, 1995, sermon, 30:10, accessed on March 2, 2017, online at *gospelinlife.com/adoration-hallowed-be-thy-name-6391*

5. Angie Smith, *Seamless: Understanding the Bible as One Complete Story* (Nashville: LifeWay Press, 2015), 28.

6. Ibid., Cloud and Townsend, *Safe People: How to Find Relationships That Are Good for You and Avoid Those That Aren't* (Grand Rapids: Zondervan, 1995), 63-64.

7. Ibid., 65.

8. Joe Rigney, "When Envy Turns Deadly," *Desiring God blog*, April 16, 2014, accessed

March 1, 2017. Available online at *desiringgod. org/articles/when-envy-turns-deadly*

9. Henry Hampton Halley, *Halley's Bible Handbook with the New International Version* (Grand Rapids: Zondervan, 2000), accessed via *mywsb.com.*

10. John MacArthur, *The MacArthur Bible Commentary* (Nashville: Thomas Nelson, 2005), accessed via *mywsb.com.*

Week 5

1. Daniel Goleman, *Social Intelligence: The New Science of Human Relationships* (New York: Bantam Dell, 2006), 308.

2. Tremper Longman III and David E. Garland, ed., *The Expositor's Bible Commentary, Revised Edition, Volume 9: Matthew & Mark* (Grand Rapids: Zondervan, 2010), 612, accessed via *mywsb.com.*

3. "HELPS Word-studies," accessed March 1, 2017, *http://biblehub.com/greek/2083.htm* copyright © 1987, 2011 by Helps Ministries, Inc.

4. Tremper Longman III and David E. Garland, ed., *The Expositor's Bible Commentary, Revised Edition, Volume 10: Luke-Acts* (Grand Rapids: Zondervan, 2007), 324, accessed online at *mywsb.com.*

5. Ibid, Goleman, 308.

6. Beth Moore, *Get Out of That Pit: Straight Talk about God's Deliverance* (Nashville: Thomas Nelson, 2007), 31.

7. Ibid, 33.

8. Ibid.

9. Ibid, 45.

10. Ibid, 47.

11. Ibid, Goleman, 308.

Week 6

1. Kenneth L. Baker, ed., *NIV Study Bible* (Grand Rapids: Zondervan, 2008), accessed online at *mywsb.com.*

2. Ibid.

3. Edwin A. Blum and Jeremy Royal Howard, ed., *HCSB Study Bible* (Nashville: Holman Bible Publishers, 2010), accessed online at *mywsb.com.*

4. Ibid, note on Galatians 6:3-5.

5. Ibid, Cloud and Townsend, 97.

6. Ibid, 189.

7. Ibid, 189-190.

8. Ibid, 190.

9. Oswald Chambers, *Utmost: Classic Readings and Prayers from Oswald Chambers* (Grand Rapids: Discovery House Publishers, 2012), 21.

10. Ibid, Cloud and Townsend, 197.

11. Ibid., 72-73.

12. Adapted from the list created by Drs. Cloud and Townsend, *Safe People,* 190-195.

13. Ibid, 182-184.

COME AS YOU ARE,
AND FIND YOURSELF AMONG FRIENDS.

BE ENCOURAGED. Take a moment to breathe by beginning each day with a passage of Scripture and a story of everyday faith from this collection of 365 devotions written by women whose stories echo your own.

AVAILABLE WHEREVER BOOKS ARE SOLD.

HELP GIRLS EXPLORE THE BIBLICAL FOUNDATION OF FRIENDSHIP

— A BIBLE STUDY FOR TEEN GIRLS —

WE SAVED YOU A SEAT

Finding and Keeping Lasting Friendships

(in)courage community manager

LISA-JO BAKER

LifeWay | Girls

We Saved You A Seat is a seven-session study that looks at the heart of lasting friendships. It reminds girls that friendship takes vulnerability, service, and forgiveness. It's learning to exercise joy instead of jealousy and encouragement instead of envy. In friendship, sometimes we need to be willing to go first – whether we're the new girl in a circle of friends or we've been part of the same group since elementary school.

AVAILABLE AT LIFEWAY.COM/GIRLS

LifeWay | Girls

But what if we knew we could never be unfriended? Would we risk friendship then?

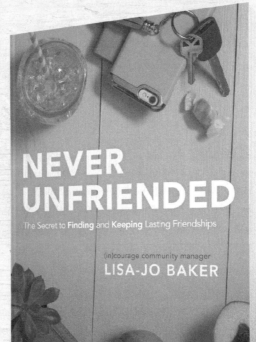

Starting with that guarantee from the most faithful friend who ever lived – Jesus – this book is a step-by-step guide to friendships you can trust.

NeverUnfriended.com